THE MOST S
PLACI
ON EARTH

The story of the East Anglian village of Elveden and the birth of the world's first tanks

✦✛✛✛✛✦

Best wishes,

Roger Pugh

Roger Pugh

Foreword by Lord Iveagh

Larks Press

Published by the Larks Press
Ordnance Farmhouse, Guist Bottom, Dereham NR20 5PF
01328 829207
larks.press@xlnmail.com

To my incomparable wife Clare
and our deeply-loved family,
in the hope that our wonderful
grandchildren, Alexandra, Krishan and Sonali, will
see a world in which the design, development,
manufacture and use of weapons is increasingly rejected.

EXPRESSIONS OF GRATITUDE

The author would like to express his sincere thanks for the help he has
received from:
The Tank Museum at Bovington, David Fletcher and
Katie Thompson in particular
The Imperial War Museum, London, Parveen Sohdi in particular
The Liddell Hart Centre for Military Archives, King's College, London
The Suffolk Record Office, Bury St. Edmunds,
Victoria Goodwin in particular
David Addy and his superb 'St. Edmundsbury Chronicle' website
Mr Daniel Tatnell for the plan of the site
Rev. Sue Nutt of the parish church of St Gregory, Barnham
The poem 'Blighters' is reproduced by kind permission of the estate of
George Sassoon, © Siegfried Sassoon
Finally, a very special expression of gratitude to my elder son, Tim Pugh, for
making all the arrangements for our visit to Flers and our tour of the Somme
battlefields, for chauffeuring me, and for providing great companionship and
organizational abilities throughout!

British Library Cataloguing-in-Publication Data
A catalogue record for this book is available
from the British Library

Copyright © Roger Pugh 2014

ISBN 9781 904006 76 3

FOREWORD

Nearly a hundred years have gone by since the Elveden estate was the home of what was then the most important military installation in the world – the British Army's training ground for its revolutionary new weapon, the tank. Completely concealed from prying eyes, the novel and intimidating machines roared, wallowed and smashed their way across twenty-five square miles of a replica Western Front battlefield created here in Suffolk, spitting fire from their machine guns and cannons as they did so and giving rise to their first commander's personal nickname for them: Dragons.

I am proud that when asked to give up so much of his land for this crucial national purpose, my forebear, the Lord Iveagh, did so immediately and unhesitatingly – though, as the ensuing account records, for some months it was revealed not even to him what his land was being used for!

Now, almost a century later, in the mind's eye it still remains possible - especially on a misty early morning or when dusk is falling - to see the ghosts of those machines and their crews preparing for what we still, and rightly, call the Great War.

Given my family background, I'm prone to imagine that as those young and brave men endured the nigh-unbearable heat and noise inside their pioneering machines, thoughts of a cool Guinness must have sometimes crossed their minds. If so, I do devoutly hope that the war-torn world of 1916 afforded them at least the small and homely comfort of a pint or two before they departed for the horrors of battle in France, where sadly so many of them still lie.

Edward Guinness
4th Earl of Iveagh

Elveden 2014

3

PROLOGUE

Every day, thousands of motorists travel along that part of the busy A11 road which runs through the Suffolk parish of Elveden. But few if any realise, as they head north to Norwich and the north Norfolk coast, or south to London and the Midlands (or simply turn off to stay at the nearby Center Parcs holiday complex), that stretching before them is a tract of land on which – for good or ill – the face of modern warfare was changed forever.

For it was here, in the spring, summer and autumn of 1916, that twenty-five square miles of heathland were used as the first training ground for a revolutionary British secret weapon – the tank.

World war had been raging for a year-and-a-half. Casualties were already immense. The new 30-ton monsters, it was hoped, would bring victory, or, at any rate, greatly contribute to it. Thus knowledge of their existence had to be kept from the German Army and its allies at all costs, lest the crucial element of surprise be lost. Consequently, the training ground for the new weapon was, as recorded by an officer at the time, 'more closely circled than the Sleeping Beauty's palace, more zealously guarded than the Paradise of a Shah'.

In short, the Elveden Explosives Area, to use its deliberately misleading cover name, became for much of 1916 *the most secret place on Earth.*

In this little book we shall follow the birth of the tank, the story of the secret training ground, the tank crews who came there, how they were trained, and what happened to them when they first went into battle.

ONE

The Birth of the Tank

For some months after the outbreak of war in early August 1914 the fighting on the Western Front between France and Britain on the one hand and Germany on the other, though massive in scale, was fluid and fought in open countryside. But by Christmas the front had become largely static, stretching in unbroken trench lines from Belgium to the Swiss border.

It was already clear to some military thinkers that machine guns, artillery, trenches, concreted strongpoints and bunkers, combined with belts of barbed wire as much as thirty metres deep, constituted a defensive combination almost impossible for attacking troops to assault successfully. Consequently, one or two military minds in Britain were already turning to the need for a new weapon to give attacking troops a better chance of breaking through. Prominent amongst them was a Royal Engineers officer, Lieutenant-Colonel E. D. (Ernest Dunlop) Swinton.

In the Boer War (1899-1902) Swinton had experimented with running armoured trains across the South African veldt and at the outbreak of the World War he was appointed Deputy Director of Railways for the British Expeditionary Force (the BEF) in France. Almost immediately he noted the success with which the BEF was already employing armoured cars. In essence these were conversions of Rolls Royce civilian car chassis, which retained conventional wheels and tyres, but were fitted with light armour and machine guns. Curiously, all such vehicles belonged to the Royal Navy and were manned by naval personnel, their original purpose having been to protect naval shore facilities and to rescue naval airmen shot down over land.

In October 1914, Swinton's reflections on his experiences led him to prepare a lengthy memorandum proposing the creation of motor-powered machines mounted on caterpillar tracks to provide cross-country capability, equipped with more heavily armoured bodywork and carrying cannons or machine guns or a combination of the two. Such machines, he suggested, would greatly assist in breaking through the German defences.

Because it had many similarities to the Royal Navy-operated armoured cars, Swinton's proposal for a new machine ultimately came to the attention of Winston Churchill, then First Lord of the Admiralty, the Royal Navy's ruling body. Churchill enthusiastically and immediately supported this concept of a 'land battleship' and quickly established an Admiralty project committee to take the idea forward. Thus he set in motion, under the patronage of the Royal Navy, the design and production of a weapon which could be employed nowhere but on land, and which, in practice, was to be used exclusively by the Army – an Army which had not approved or requested its development at all.

Whether or not Swinton's proposal qualifies him to be known as 'the father of the tank', as claimed by most, is not entirely certain. It seems he might not have been alone in his thinking; certainly, numerous other distinguished men – military and civilian – played crucial parts in the design, development, manufacture and deployment of the new weapon, and we shall encounter some of them in the Elveden story. But undoubtedly Swinton played a pivotal role, contributing crucial insight plus energy, drive, organising ability and visionary tactical and strategic thinking.

Of course, it was all along recognised that, being a land warfare weapon, the use of such a 'land battleship' on a large scale would at some point certainly involve the Army, and they were consulted. By June 1915 a favourable reaction was obtained from the Commander-in-Chief of the British Expeditionary Force in France (then Sir John French) and a Joint Naval and Military Committee, the 'Landships Committee', was established. A clever young Jewish banker called Albert Stern was appointed as its secretary. A defective ankle having barred Stern from a fighting role, the Navy had nevertheless recognised his administrative talents and had commissioned him as a Lieutenant. It was the Navy, too, which nominated him for the secretaryship. By virtue of this position, Stern was to become the prime coordinator throughout the war for blending together the design, development, testing and production of the new weapons, for liaising with all the military and civilian authorities involved, and for 'trouble-shooting' in every direction.

Stern's initial difficulties were manifold. His problem in even obtaining an office, seemingly a minor matter, perfectly typifies the difficulties which on every side surrounded the tank's gestation. 'No Government Department would provide any office accommodation for us', Stern recalled, 'so ... I took an office at my own expense at 83 Pall Mall and installed in it my entire organisation, which consisted of myself and Mr. Percy Anderson, at that time a petty officer in the [Navy's] Armoured Car Division.' (1) A few months later, his staff by now having grown, Stern managed, at Government expense at last, to obtain more commodious office accommodation in the Hotel Metropole. But his tenure was soon jeopardised: 'A civil servant, an Assistant Secretary, came to see me ... He told me that because my Department was of no real importance, since he had no knowledge of what it was, he had arranged that during the next Sunday all my papers and drawings were to be moved into a small flat in a back street ... ' Stern was just about to leave on a

'Little Willie' the world's first tank. A quick-witted individual saved it from destruction during a World War II scrap metal drive, claiming it could be useful for airfield defence. It is now on display at the Tank Museum, Bovington.

trip to the Army in France and told the civil servant that 'the Department could not move as it was concerned in matters of the greatest national importance, and would require, before long, a very large building of its own. This had no effect on him, so I gave instructions to one of my officers in [the civil servant's] presence to put an armed guard on my office while I was away and to resist any attack. Should he make an attempt he was to be arrested ... and tied to a stake [at the barracks] for 24 hours ... ' The offices went unmolested. (At the end of the war, Stern was knighted, but the identity of the civil servant has sunk into oblivion.)

Despite all such difficulties, various private as well as official efforts to develop a suitable fighting machine soon followed the Landship Committee's formation. By far the most significant of these was the design and manufacture of 'Little Willie' by William Foster and Company Limited, agricultural engineers of Lincoln. This was done under the direction of William (later Sir William) Tritton, the company's managing director, greatly assisted by W.G. Wilson, a highly talented engineer who, like Albert Stern, had become a wartime officer in the Royal Navy's armoured car division. To ensure secrecy and to minimise interruptions during Little Willie's gestation, Tritton and Wilson, accompanied by Foster's chief draughts-man, William Rigby, separated themselves from the factory and for several weeks spent their days and evenings – and frequently their nights – in a secure room at the White Hart Hotel in Lincoln. (This room is known today as the 'Tank Room'.) Perhaps the most crucial of their design breakthroughs was the invention of a new form of caterpillar track; experiments had proved that no existing form of track was capable of performing satisfactorily in military conditions. Their revolutionary track was made from pressed steel plate; it was light and strong, and, above all, highly resistant to detaching itself from its runners.

The vehicle which emerged, the aforesaid Little Willie, constituted the first tank in the form we know it today and was named derisively after the German Kaiser, Wilhelm, a man of less than impressive physical stature, or possibly in jocular reference to William Tritton, who was physically a very big man and was looked upon by many as Little Willie's 'father'. Little Willie weighed 16.5 tonnes and was just over 8 metres in length (26 feet 6 inches), 2.51 metres (9 feet) in height and 2.86 metres (9 feet 5 inches) in width. It was intended for a crew of six and had provision for a 2-pounder Vickers gun as its main armament and six Madsen machine guns as secondary.

However, even as Little Willie was being tested and modified and found wanting in the light of experience, another and altogether more ambitious machine, known as 'Big Willie', was already being designed by the same trio to meet a revised War Office requirement. This specified that the new weapon must be capable of crossing an 8-feet wide trench and of climbing a parapet 4 feet 6 inches high (typical dimensions for German defensive works on the Western Front at that time).

Big Willie formed the basis of what was to become the first production model tank (the 'Mark One'). Big Willie was characterised by its instantly recognisable lozenge-shaped or rhomboidal profile, and its tracks ran round the complete longitudinal exterior of the hull. This prototype – also known as the 'Wilson Machine' or 'Centipede' – was, like Little Willie, built in Foster's works. (Soon afterwards, the various nicknames for this second and much more sophisticated machine were to be abandoned in favour of 'Mother', in reference to 'her' being so much bigger than Little Willie and thus akin to 'his' mother.)

After some preliminary runs in a secluded part of Burton Park in Lincoln, Mother was more extensively tested on 29th January 1916 in a remote area of the vast grounds of Hatfield House in Hertfordshire. (This is the ancestral home of the Cecil family and in those days neither the house nor the grounds were open to the public.) Trials continued there for the next few weeks and some demonstrations were given to VIPs. David Lloyd-George, then the Minister of Munitions and to become Prime Minister later in the war, witnessed one of them. In his War Memoirs he wrote: 'The experiment was a complete success, the tank achieving even more than it was asked to accomplish. And I can recall the feeling of delighted amazement with which I saw for the first time the ungainly monster, bearing the inscription "H.M.S. Centipede" on its breast, plough through thick entanglements, wallow through deep mud, and

'Mother' the prototype for the Mark One tanks which went into action at Flers-Courcelette, shown here on trials at Hatfield Park. The figure with the walking stick is probably Lord Salisbury, the owner of the Park.

heave its huge bulk over parapets and across trenches. Mr. Balfour's delight [Balfour had succeeded Churchill as First Lord of the Admiralty] was as great as my own, and it was only with some difficulty that some of us persuaded him to disembark from H.M. Landship whilst she crossed the last trench, a trench several feet wide.' (2) Balfour and Lloyd George were yet to realise that the path from successful demonstration to ultimate battlefield success would be a long one ...

Forty machines were promptly ordered, increased to 100 shortly thereafter. Twenty-five of this first batch were to be built by Fosters at Lincoln and seventy-five by the Metropolitan Carriage, Wagon and Finance Company of Birmingham. In April the order was increased yet again, to 150.

There were two versions of the Mark 1, the 'Male' and the

'Female'. As main armament, the Male was equipped with two six-pounder Hotchkiss guns, the Female with four Vickers .303 machine guns. These weapons were mounted in projecting sponsons (enclosed, armoured gun platforms) on either side of the tank. In addition, both versions carried a forward-firing machine gun. Fitting the weaponry in sponsons (a naval term) rather than in a revolving turret, enabled fire to be directed downwards into trenches at a sharp angle unachievable by a turret.

The Male weighed 28.4 tonnes, the Female a tonne less. Both types were powered by a Daimler-Knight 6-cylinder engine of 16 litres capacity producing 105 horsepower. The more heavily-armed Male was for use against strongpoints, bunkers, enemy artillery and the like, the machine-gun-equipped Female for use principally against trenches and infantry. Both versions were equally effective in the vital tasks of flattening wire and breaking through barricades, and thus their roles were to a considerable extent interchangeable. (However, the bigger demand in course of time from front-line soldiers proved to be for the machine-gun-armed Female, and of the 2,200 British heavy tanks manufactured in the course of the war about 1,300 were Female.)

What one might paradoxically term a mystifyingly obvious early defect of the design was the gravity-fed fuel tank, vulnerably located above the heads of the commander and driver, perfectly positioned to rain 44 gallons of burning petrol directly on to them in the event of its being hit. This was fairly smartly altered to a fuel tank located much more securely at the rear of the vehicle and feeding the supply to the engine by means of a pump.

This account is routinely using the word 'tank' as something the reader will be completely familiar with in a military context, but this was not always the case. In fact, it was not until the first order for large-scale production was placed in February 1916 (as recounted above) that the word grew to mean a weapon of war. The prototype vehicles, Little Willie and Mother, had been constructed by a small, hand-picked team. But how was secrecy to be maintained when mass production began and very large numbers of engineers and workmen would need to be involved, men who would soon see the purpose of the beasts they were constructing, men to whom no convincing cover story could be given to divert them from the truth? The only possible decision was taken: simply to tell the workforce the truth and to swear each member of it, individually and solemnly, not to reveal to anyone, under any circumstances, what was going on. This faith proved amply justified and it is remarkable to record that so far as is known, not a single man ever broke his trust.

However, a difficulty remained: what were the members of the workforce actually to reply when asked (as they inevitably would be) by family, friends or in the pub, 'What are you working on at the factory nowadays?' To say simply, 'I'm not allowed to tell you – it's a secret,' would do nothing but stimulate an inquirer's interest. And if rumours that there was a hidden 'something' ever reached German ears, the enemy would be instantly alerted to the fact that here was a mystery which needed investigating. So the men were told to reply that they were building large water tanks for use by the Army in Mesopotamia - where the British army was fighting the Turks and water was indeed in short supply! This worked wonderfully well, and soon the single word 'tank' was in use as a common code word. (Other, deliberately conflicting ruses were also employed to 'muddy the waters' – for example, 'With Care To Petrograd' was painted in large Cyrillic letters on both sides of each machine in case one of them should be accidentally spotted by an 'outsider'.

(Totally unforeseen at the time was the fact that in 1919 tanks would indeed be supplied to Russia, for use by the White Army in its struggle against the Reds.)

A Mark One being loaded at Lincoln for delivery to Elveden. Note the deliberately misleading Cyrillic script. Ironically, in 1918 and 1919, Britain did supply tanks to Russia for supply to the White Army against the Communist revolution.

All this is not to say that there were never any 'leaks' from any source whatsoever. Swinton tells of a personal experience he had a little later: '... a charming lady, my neighbour at a luncheon party, on hearing my name began artlessly to ply me with questions, which showed that someone had been talking unwisely. I remembered that a certain young officer [of the tanks] bore her name and made a shrewd guess at their relationship. Very seriously, and in a low tone, I told her there was only one person from whom she could have learned what she knew; that if it got out it would not only mean his death but the death of many others and possibly the loss of the War; that unless she promised to maintain silence, except to contradict anything she had already divulged, I would order that individual's arrest by telephone and have him tried by court-martial for treachery, the penalty for which was death. Greatly upset, the lady vowed she would carry out my instructions.' (3)

Despite this alarming incident, the innumerable and understandably obsessive precautions taken to preserve secrecy were to prove completely effective overall. The Germans were to learn nothing of the tanks' existence until the moment they rumbled towards their trenches and opened fire.

Colonel Ernest Dunlop Swinton, generally regarded as 'the Father of the Tank'. He proposed and oversaw the development of the first tanks and created the Elveden 'battlefield' where he directed the training of the first tank crews

TWO

The Men

As we have seen, the first large-scale production order for tanks was placed in February 1916. It was by now acknowledged by all concerned that, despite the early initiatives having been taken by the Navy, the only sensible long-term solution was to incorporate the first tanks and their successors wholly into the army, for clearly it was as an integral part of the army that the tanks would have to be employed. The earliest men recruited to operate them were therefore drafted into the 'Motor Cycle Machine Gun Service', an Army unit which, as the name indicates, carried machine-guns on motor-cycles equipped with sidecars. However, a special new unit, which absorbed the motorcyclists, was formed in March, designated the 'Heavy Section, Machine Gun Corps' – a name chosen, of course, to continue to disguise the true nature of what was afoot.

Unsurprisingly, Colonel Swinton was appointed to command the new unit. His immediate priorities were to recruit suitable personnel and to find and develop a training ground so that he could marshal the tanks and the yet-to-be-recruited men into an effective fighting force.

The War Office, or the part of it that recognized that tanks were a serious innovation, had already circulated to commanding officers of selected Army units a suitably obscure request for potential tank officers, headed 'Strictly Secret and Confidential'. It read:

'Volunteers are required for an exceedingly dangerous and hazardous duty of a secret nature. Officers who have been awarded decorations for bravery, and are experienced in the handling of men, and with an engineering background, should have their names submitted to this office.'

This, of course, brought forth a useful crop. But in mid-April the process was widened and accelerated by selecting men suitable for commissioning as tank officers with a speed and informality which seems hardly credible today, typical though it was of wartime conditions.

First, Swinton went to Chelsea Barracks and in a single morning selected about thirty officer cadets with some mechanical knowledge. Knowing that there were in the universities a large number of undergraduates anxious to contribute to the war effort, on the following morning Swinton and his colleague Colonel Bradley went to Oxford University and recruited fifty more volunteers, again mainly ones with some mechanical knowledge. Shortly thereafter he swooped on Cambridge University, where he 'bagged' another fifty. In short order, all these men were called together at Wellington Barracks where Swinton gave them an address about what lay ahead. One recruit, 26-year-old Lieutenant Vic Huffam, recalled that Swinton 'warned us that we had volunteered for a very dangerous mission and said if any man had doubts he was to step back one pace'. Nobody moved and Huffam, in common with the rest, soon found himself a Lieutenant in the 'Heavy Section' - a name which, he said, still gave him and his comrades 'no clue whatsoever as to our real unit!' (1)

Huffam was a native of Heaton Chapel, near Stockport, Cheshire, but no one had to undertake a longer journey than he did to join up, travelling as he did all the way back from the Western Australian goldfields. He had worked there for seven years as a technician and agent for the engineering firm of

Crossley.(2) Initially he had been commissioned as a 2nd Lieutenant in the Royal Norfolk Regiment but had had his attention drawn to the Heavy Section by the War Office circular. Though excited by the prospect of the dangerous unknown that lay ahead of him, it was with mixed feelings that he left his existing duties as a company commander in the Norfolks: '[The company comprised] two hundred regular soldiers, some twice my age. They had seen service in France and were being trained to go back. They were, I would say, the toughest bunch of old sweats one could have, tougher than some of the Australian miners I had known, but we got on, and I shall remember as long as I live their bearing on the parade ground before I marched them to the station en route to France.' Huffam was soon to be appointed as commander of Dolly, Tank D9, where his experience in the Norfolks stood him in good stead. We shall return to his story later.

For recruiting potential NCOs and other ranks the editor of *The Motor Cycle* magazine was approached and advertisements for mechanically-minded men were inserted. Gunner William Dawson, a 28-year-old from Boston in Lincolnshire, was one of many who replied; he was accepted into the Motor Cycle Machine Gun Corps after an interview in Coventry. The magazine's editor, Geoffrey Smith, also proved useful in putting out 'feelers' to his personal contacts – though not, of course, himself knowing what it was he was inviting them to get involved in.

Simultaneously, swarms of clerks were set combing Service records to identify suitably-qualified NCOs and other ranks already in the Army or Navy, wherever they were serving. A number of tank gunners, for example, were drawn from the Navy because the 6-pounder Hotchkiss gun with which the Male tanks were to be fitted was, essentially, a naval weapon.

One suitable potential driver, Sergeant (then Corporal) Robert Parker was tracked down in France. Parker had previously had engineering experience in the nascent aircraft industry and after that had been a private chauffeur and mechanic. He had also had experience driving Holt caterpillar tractors. In the Spring of 1916, Parker was the commander of one of these, assisted by a crew of two. He and his men were in France pulling a 9.2 inch howitzer toward what was to become the battlefield of the Somme when a staff car pulled up nearby. In an interview in the 1970s, Parker described what happened next: '[T]he staff officer called my boys ... and asked for Corporal Parker, and they said "He's driving". "All right, stop him," so they stopped me and I got down and they told me that this staff officer wanted me. I went back and spoke to him at the car and he said "What's your number?" I said "MS2934". He said "That's right, get your kit".'

'Well, we used to stow our kit up in the corrugated iron roof of the caterpillar so I got that down, went back to the car with it, he said "Get in". I said "What about my two boys, what are they going to do?" He said "They'll have to go on their own, we'll notify the Battery". So I got in the car and went up to Boulogne and then down to Le Havre with him, and there I was given charge of thirty caterpillar men from other batteries all along the line, and they embarked us in a Clyde paddle steamer and we came home to Southampton on the paddle steamer.' (3)

History does not record how the abandoned tractor and 9.2 howitzer and Parker's two men finally reached the Somme or the reaction or language of the officers awaiting their arrival. It does record that neither Parker nor his thirty companions were told why they were required, simply that it was 'a special job'; like almost everyone else, they first learned of new weapons called tanks only when they reached their final destination.

The disparate group of officers and men identified by these various methods was temporarily assembled at the unwelcomingly named Siberia Camp in Surrey and organised into six companies, lettered A through to F inclusive. Each company was to be composed of twenty-five tanks (one of them a reserve), divided into four sections of six and further divided into sub-sections of two. A company was commanded by a major, a section by a captain. Thus the total strength of a company was thirty-one officers and about two hundred other ranks.

Such training as took place in Surrey was largely confined to the maintenance and firing of the 6-pounder guns with which the Male tanks were to be fitted (carried out at the nearby Bisley Rifle Range) and to the maintenance and firing of machine-guns. As noted, the 6-pounder was a naval gun, so instructors and a cadre of gunners from the Royal Navy were seconded to or joined the tank service for this purpose – in other words, moved from a sea-going service which had been in existence for hundreds of years to a land force which had been in existence for not a hundred days. However, as there were as yet no tanks for the guns to be fitted to, this early stage of weapons training could not accurately represent the conditions of firing whilst on the move, nor under the very difficult environment expected to prevail in the tanks' interiors.

In addition to recruiting men, Swinton's other priority was to find land, a very large amount of it, on which he could develop a training ground where comprehensive instruction and practice in all aspects of the new weapon could be given as soon as the tanks started rolling off the production line.

This he now set about doing.

THREE

The Search for the 'Battlefield'

After making inquiries through War Office channels, Swinton found the right man to help him in his search for land in the shape of an officer called Major Tandy of the Royal Engineers. Tandy had previously been employed by the Survey of India, the Indian equivalent of the UK Ordnance Survey. Having already served in France, where he had been wounded, Tandy was now fit for light duties. Swinton records how he and Tandy urgently set about inspecting countryside around the army heartland of Aldershot and elsewhere but soon found themselves at a loss to identify terrain both suitable for the purpose *and* capable of being secured from prying eyes.

Swinton instructed Tandy to cast the net wider, and in the first week of April 1916 Tandy sent Swinton a telegram from the town of Thetford in Norfolk, saying he had found the ideal place a few miles away. (It is an interesting historical coincidence that it was at Thetford in 1856 that a steam-driven machine known as the Burrell-Boyden 'Endless Railway Machine' was built at the St Nicholas Traction Engine Works, almost certainly the first vehicle in the world to incorporate the principle of self-laying tracks, the fundamental feature of the tank.)

Tandy's proposed site was just over the Norfolk county border, at Elveden in Suffolk. The nature of the surface there and the mildly undulating contours rendered it highly suitable for tank training. It was also readily accessible by road and railway yet at the same time almost completely hidden in practically deserted countryside. (It must be remembered that Thetford Forest, now a predominant feature of the landscape,

23

did not then exist; it was planted, largely as a work-creation scheme, in the 1920s and 1930s.) Swinton immediately caught a train for Thetford, endorsed Tandy's conclusions, and contacted the landowner, Lord Iveagh of the Guinness dynasty. Though more than a little appalled at losing some of his finest shooting territory, not to say valuable farmland, Lord Iveagh promptly agreed to co-operate in the national interest even though, naturally, Swinton could not divulge to him the reason for the land being required.

Elveden Hall, the seat of Lord Iveagh who surrendered 25 square miles of his land for the 'Elveden Explosives Area'. The Officers' mess of the new tank arm found its home in the stables.

Swinton then swiftly obtained the invaluable services of Mr Driver Jonas, a civilian estate agent temporarily attached to the Lands Branch of the War Office. Jonas promised that he would immediately visit Lord Iveagh, arrange for compensation and obtain entry within a week. Swinton, though himself habituated to cutting corners in the interest of speed, was profoundly doubtful that Jonas could fulfil his promise, but Jonas was as good as his word; Lord Iveagh was keen to help, and the deal was done in a matter of days. (The possibility of compulsory requisitioning, apparently, did not need to be mentioned.) Thus the world's first tank training ground became available almost immediately. Swinton was much impressed by Jonas's speedy achievement and gave him some words of advice: 'You are a civilian now. Remain so. You can enter a room in [the War Office], say what you think and get attention. In your own line you are an expert. What you say goes. But once you put on uniform you'll only be a junior officer, you'll have to stand to attention while your seniors in rank sit down and tell you how to run your own show.' (Unfortunately, despite holding out for some months, Jonas was eventually forced to take a commission and, says Swinton, 'like Samson was at once shorn of his strength'. But Jonas's name still lives on in 'Carter Jonas', specialists in estate agency, commercial property and rural land and businesses.)

According to a local guidebook published a few years before the war, the countryside in and around Elveden was then 'some of the wildest and least populated land in East Anglia, with many square miles uncultivated and unenclosed'. It was possible in parts 'to walk eight or ten miles without seeing more than one or two houses ....' (1) Swinton described the area, apart from a few wooded segments, as 'desolate'.

The twenty-five square mile parcel of land took in several farms, the principal ones being Bernersfield Farm, Canada Farm, North Stow Farm, Culford Lodge Farm, Lodge Farm, West Farm and New Farm. These included farmhouses and farm workers' cottages and every inhabitant had to move to alternative homes outside the area with almost no prior warning.

North Stow Farmhouse, the centre of a 'German' redoubt, under repair after damage by tank gunfire.

North Stow Farmhouse today (2014)

The approximate boundaries of the area were, to the north, a four-mile segment of a track known as Duke's Ride; to the east, the Thetford-to-Bury St Edmunds road (now the A134); to the west, the Thetford-to-Mildenhall Road (now the busy A11 trunk route); and to the south on a line running from below Canada Farm and thence back again to the Thetford-to-Bury St Edmunds road. (See map on p.30.)

As there was no road vehicle capable of carrying a tank at that time, an indispensable asset of the site was, as noted earlier, its proximity to the railway network, which enabled the delivery of the tanks direct from factories in Lincoln and Birmingham. Great Eastern Railway's Bury St Edmunds -to- Thetford line ran along the site's eastern boundary and at its northernmost point, Thetford Bridge Station, it joined Great Eastern's Cambridge line. Via the latter, access to the whole national network was available. There was, too, a handily-placed station at Barnham, about two-and-a-half miles south of Thetford Bridge. Both Thetford Bridge and Barnham stations, but predominantly the former, featured heavily in the transport of troops to and from the site. As we shall see, these existing railway facilities were not quite good enough and it was foreseen that a massive siding and ramp would have to be constructed alongside the training ground to enable the tanks to be unloaded and re-loaded.

Occupation of Lord Iveagh's land having been secured, work was immediately put in hand to create the training facilities. This had to be done in conditions of the greatest secrecy. Even in the Army, the only person outside the Tank organisation who knew the true purpose of the newly acquired land was the Commanding Officer of the 69th Division, Major General F. H. Kelly, whose headquarters were at Thetford. The secret was not shared even with his staff.

Swinton recorded: 'The few inhabitants having been

Thetford Bridge Railway Station just prior to its demolition in 1976. The great majority of tank crews arrived and departed from here, including those departing for the first battles.

removed, all the roads leading into the area were blocked; and it was publicly given the off-putting name "The Elveden Explosives Area".' Notices warning the public of the deadly peril of entering were prominently erected round the entire perimeter. A force of some 450 men of the Royal Defence Corps was employed for guard duties, supplemented by infantry from regiments of the line (for example men of the Hampshire Regiment), and by mounted troops, which brought the total guard force to 700. One new arrival was not a little surprised to find Indian cavalry patrolling the perimeter. This was, in fact, very appropriate, as the Elveden estate had previously been owned by Prince Duleep Singh, the last native ruler of the Punjab, who in the Victorian era had taken up residence at Elveden Hall after effectively being deprived of his Indian kingdom by the British Raj. (It is fitting to record here that more

28

than 50,000 Indian troops sacrificed their lives in the service of Britain in the First World War.)

An outer security cordon eleven miles in circumference was set up. Through this no one could pass without a permit. This was supplemented by an inner cordon and yet a third cordon within that. Swinton remembered: 'Numerous rumours about what was going on were current locally. One was that a tunnel was being bored right through to Germany, another that experiments were being conducted with some new and terrible explosive, and so forth. They were not discouraged, as any explanation, provided it were not the right one, was better than unsatisfied curiosity.'

But there was one group from whom the secret could not be kept: the pilots and observers of the Royal Flying Corps based at Snarehill Aerodrome, a mile or two to the east of Thetford, who, whenever they took to the skies, could hardly fail to notice the mysterious new vehicles below. The airmen's existence, says Swinton, was regarded at first as 'a nuisance and a danger', for it would be impossible to conceal tanks in motion from the airmen who were continually flying low overhead. 'All efforts to prevent pilots from crossing over the area proved unavailing, and so a virtue was made of necessity. Under a pledge of secrecy the nature and purpose of the Heavy Section was divulged to the local officers of the R.F.C. This eliminated unhealthy curiosity.' As we shall see, it was also soon to lead to the first example of co-operation between these two novel technological branches of the British armed services.

All in all, every conceivable step was taken to safeguard the secret. It was Lieutenant Clough Williams-Ellis (subsequently the prominent architect and creator of the famous and idiosyncratic village of Portmeirion in North Wales) who memorably summed up the precautions taken by saying that the training area was *'more closely circled than the Sleeping Beauty's palace, more zealously guarded than the Paradise of a Shah'*. (2)

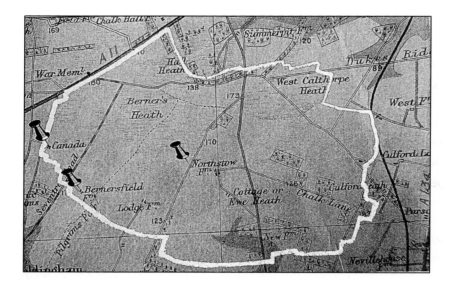

The outer perimeter of the training ground is shown here in white. Elveden Hall is just to the north-east of the site and Thetford about seven miles in the same direction.

FOUR

Creating the 'Battlefield'

➤·⊦⊦⊗⊧⊢⊦·◄

The massive task now facing the Heavy Section was to create an exact replica of a real battlefield for the tanks to practice on – a replica with especially broad and deep trenches as used by the Germans on the Somme front. The design of the 'battlefield' was carried out by Captain Martel of the Royal Engineers, specially sent over from France for the purpose. Martel had personally participated in the dangerous trade of raiding enemy trenches and had extensive experience of exploring both British and German trench lines. He was assisted by four other young Royal Engineers' officers.

Swinton recorded: 'The model battlefield was over one and a half miles in width. In depth, it included the British support and front lines, No Man's Land, the German first, support, second and third lines. It was as complete a copy of the real thing as time, experience, labour and money could make it. It comprised breastworks, wire entanglements, abatis (barriers of felled trees), shell craters, communication trenches, dugouts, machine-gun emplacements and nests, magazines, grenade stores, in fact every sort of work which, according to the latest information, might be met with in the defensive zone. The various signposts behind the enemy line were marked in German and the men instructed in their meaning.' At least two massive craters were created by detonating explosives to simulate the blowing of underground mines, which both the British and the Germans employed as part of their offensives. North Stow Farm became a redoubt, i.e. a large, fortified strongpoint, at a tactically-important point in the 'German' lines. All in all, the quantity of materials consumed in doing all this was staggering - 1,000,000 sandbags alone. (The labour and materials needed to implement Martel's plan for this mock battlefield leave one in awe at the nigh-incredible resources needed to create the real trench line system on the Western Front, stretching as that did from the Belgian coast to the Swiss border.)

Guards of the Royal Defence Corps prepare a meal using improvised cooking equipment. Army rations were not infrequently supplemented by judicious poaching of gamebirds and rabbits.

Initially, two battalions of Pioneers from the Home Defence Force were allocated to Elveden for the task of construction, but it soon became apparent that many more men would be needed to complete the job in the required timescale. Therefore, a further Pioneer battalion, of former miners from South Wales, was hurriedly drafted in. (The battalion's commanding officer had been desperately disappointed to discover that the 'urgent reinforcements' he commanded were destined for Suffolk and not the Western Front; whether his men shared his disappointment we do not know.) Thus it was that 3,000 men spent six weeks labouring from dawn to dusk, in all weathers, to create an accurate representation of the alien world in which the tank men would soon find themselves in action. (In addition to enabling the timetable to be met, the advent of the Welsh miners brought about a marked, if temporary, improvement in the standard of British Army singing round the evening campfires, with hymn tunes and traditional Welsh ballads supplementing roughly-sung Army favourites such as 'Mademoiselle from Armentières', 'Tipperary' and 'We'll Wash your Dirty Daughter'.)

Some of the men of the Pioneer Corps pose for a photograph. It took 3,000 of them six weeks to create the 'battlefield'.

The complexity and depth of the defences adopted by the German Army on the Western Front, and by the British too, is brought home by the plan of just a part of the replica battlefield (see back cover). There were always at least three lines of trenches to provide defence in depth. These were dug in a zigzag pattern, thus creating 'bays', so that if a shell or grenade detonated in one bay, the adjoining bays were, hopefully, sheltered at least partly from the blast. Because of the virtual impossibility of surface journeys from one trench line to another, lateral communication trenches had to be provided on a commensurate scale. The systems became very complex when added to by the usual multiplicity of dugouts, strongpoints, machine-gun posts and redoubts which were essential to any strong defence. It was easy to get lost, especially at night, and great resilience was required to negotiate the frequently muddy and, often, flooded routes, particularly when carrying heavy loads.

In general, the Germans constructed much deeper dugouts and underground bunkers than the British or French, with much higher standards of protection from shell-fire and, usually, much-superior comfort. German bunkers could be as deep as forty feet below ground and not infrequently were fitted with electric lighting. (This more sophisticated approach of the Germans was largely because they held a dominant position strategically by having conquered and occupied so much of France and Belgium in the first months of hostilities; this to a great extent enabled them simply to let the British and French dash themselves against the rocks of the German defences. Conversely, to succeed in their aims, the Allies had to drive the Germans back to their homeland. Thus the Allies always tended to treat their own positions as only temporary, prior to what was hoped would be an all-conquering advance.)

FIVE
Elveden: the men and the machines

➤⊹⊹⊹⊹⊹⊹◄

In addition to the creation of the replica battlefield, a further priority for Swinton and his team was the construction of the railway siding referred to earlier, for the unloading and loading of tanks. This needed to be 700 feet long and have a suitable ramp. The selected site was a spur to the north-west off the railway line near Culford Lodge Farm. Swinton tells us: 'The construction of this private siding in ordinary times would have been hedged about with all sorts of restrictions. An official of the Board of Trade estimated that if the usual regulations [had been] complied with it would [have] been six weeks before it was built.' But 'red tape was cut through, ordinary procedure short-circuited, and the work carried out by the engineering department of the Great Eastern Railway, assisted by the troops on the spot, in about a week'. A huge length of tarpaulin screening was erected to shield the siding from the track. (On the rail journeys themselves, every tank had its own voluminous cover to obviate all efforts by the curious to ascertain what was within.)

The first two companies transferred from Siberia Camp to train at Elveden were C and D; their transfer took place in the last days of May and the first days of June. The men disembarked at Thetford Bridge Railway station. One of them was Lieutenant Vic Huffam, whom we met earlier and by now a tank commander in D Company. As Huffam left the station he would have seen, dominating the landscape a few hundred metres to the south, Thetford's castle mound, one of the biggest in the country and constructed by the Norman French shortly after their invasion of England in 1066. Huffam and his companions were now embarking on the first steps of a journey to help liberate the descendants of those very conquerors; thus does the wheel of history turn full circle.

Huffam and his companions had to march out to their billets at Elveden. Their enjoyment of the march was not enhanced by the torrential rain which fell for the whole seven miles. Huffam recalled that the final part of their trek took them 'through a little white gate up a lane'. (The successor to that gate, and the now-metalled lane, can still be seen just off the busy A11 trunk road.)

The modern successor to the white gate through which Lieutenant Vic Huffam and his men passed to Canada Farm after marching seven miles in the rain

Unit Headquarters were set up at Bernersfield Farm, five miles (8 kilometres) south-east of Elveden Hall. Bernersfield was also used as the base for C Company. D Company's base was the nearby Canada Farm. Tented encampments were set up and the existing houses, cottages and barns in and around the area were also used as accommodation, for the area was swamped not only with tank men as such but with large numbers of supporting personnel.

C Company was commanded by the only Sandhurst-trained officer, Major Allen Holford-Walker from Southend-on-Sea, 26 years old and the son of a Royal Artillery officer. D was commanded by the much older Major Frank Summers who was aged 44, and pretty 'long in the tooth' by Army standards. He had already seen action in Belgium, France and in the Dardanelles.

Both companies drew their officers and men from every part of the UK: to take examples at random, 2nd Lieutenant Andrew Henderson was from Perth, Gunner William Higgs from Barnstable in Devon, Lance Corporal John Farquharson from Aberdeen, Gunner Charles Hewitt from Bristol, Lieutenant Charles Wheeler-Price from Brecon in Wales, Captain Harold Mortimore from Chiswick in London and Lieutenant Arthur Blowers from Saxmundham in Suffolk. Huffam was not the only recruit re-acclimatising himself to England after returning from a life he had established overseas; others included Londoner, Lieutenant Bill Brannon, a returnee from South Africa, and a Norfolk man, Captain Stephen Sellick, who had come all the way back from China.

Backgrounds were equally diverse: from officers and men who before the war had served in the Regular Army to a peace-time theatrical producer, and a corn miller whose family had carried on their milling business in the New Forest for five generations. Gunner Lawrence Rowntree was the grandson of Joseph Rowntree the chocolate manufacturer. In conformity with his family's Quaker traditions, he had earlier served for ten months as a volunteer in the pacifist Friends Ambulance Unit but, for whatever reason, and no doubt to the perplexity and distress of his family, he subsequently enlisted in the Heavy Section.

At least two men were sons of immigrants, very new Britons indeed: Squadron Quartermaster Sergeant Harry Jacobs, born of a Russian father and a Polish mother; and Lance Corporal Charles Jung, the son of an immigrant Silesian brick-maker and his wife Sarah. One man, Gunner Victor Toombs, could hardly have been more local, hailing as he did from North Terrace, Mildenhall, just a mile or two down the road from Elveden.

Headquarters and office accommodation was largely found from existing buildings. The Officers' Mess found a home in the stables at Elveden Hall. The principal Men's Mess was in a large shed previously used for drying tobacco as part of an ultimately unsuccessful experiment by Lord Iveagh to grow the crop in this country.

Though some men were able to live in vacated farm cottages and the like, huge tented encampments had to be erected, the biggest of them at New Farm. Some locations were better than others: in his accommodation at Canada Farm, Corporal Harold Sanders, soon to be a gearsman in Lieutenant Huffam's tank, and his comrades had to contend with 'countless thousands of earwigs which stormed into our tents, clothes and kitbags'. (1)

The first two tanks to arrive at Elveden were the prototypes 'Little Willie' and 'Mother', the latter arriving on the 4th June. The first production machine arrived on the 18th June, twenty more by the 10th July and thirty more rapidly thereafter. There was thus a strength of fifty-plus by the middle of July. Naturally, the newly-arrived and arriving troops were impatient to get their hands on them. The men, recorded Captain Frank Mitchell, had been 'keyed up to the highest pitch of excitement' and 'eagerly they [had] awaited the arrival of the mystery machines. It was rumoured that they could climb trees, swim across rivers, and hop about like kangaroos! False alarms were continually being given. Somebody would rush into a hut breathlessly announcing that he had distinctly heard the throb of a strange engine, and immediately the whole camp rushed out helter-skelter to see if the long-expected cars had come.' (2)

None of the troops ever forgot his first sighting. Private W. T. Dawson recalled: 'Early one morning we were awakened by a rumbling and rattling. In great excitement everybody rushed out and there they were – the first of the tanks passing our tents to the practice driving ground. We were almost too excited to bother about any breakfast.' (3)

Another man described going for a run through seemingly deserted woods on his second evening at the Area: 'Suddenly round the bend in a lane I heard a grinding and a grunting, and a few seconds later I was confronted by the awful apparition of a Mark One tank with its weird wheeled tail. I drew up, petrified, wondering whether this was another manifestation of the concussion which had caused me to be invalided home from France.'

Similarly, an officer called Captain Groves recalled his awe: 'On arrival in the restricted area our Company was used as infantry to hold a farm and its locality. I was in a building and we were not allowed to look out until a signal was given. I opened the top of a stable door, and there 50 yards away was a colossal monster moving along at 3 m.p.h. with guns sticking out from all sides. It really made one think.' (4)

The arrival of tanks in quantity immediately introduced officers and men to what was to become a familiar yet daunting task – unloading the tanks from the railway wagons. As soon as each batch arrived - which for security was always after nightfall - intense effort was required under the glare of acetylene lamps to get them off the train and down the ramp. They then had to be moved across to the secluded areas of Canada Farm and Bernersfield Farm before daylight. Despite the time pressure, infinite care had to be taken to ease each tank off its railway wagon and safely onto and down the ramp, there being only two inches of room to spare on either side.

Another even more arduous routine, with which the troops were soon to become unhappily familiar, was the re-attachment of the gun sponsons, for the tanks always arrived with their projecting gun sponsons un-mounted, these being carried separately on other wagons. This removal of the sponsons for rail transport was essential as otherwise trackside and bridge and tunnel clearances were insufficient both in Britain and France. Each sponson weighed more than a ton-and-a-half and when in use was secured to its parent tank by 26 large and heavy metal bolts. Despite the use of special trolleys designed to ease the job of removal and re-fitting, the process was long and difficult and burned itself into the memory of every tank man.

Major W.H.L. Watson's description vividly recalls the experience: 'The tank was driven into two shallow trenches. A stout four wheeled trolley [carrying the sponson] was run along-side and a sort of crane was fitted, to which slings were attached. The sponson was girt about with these slings and the sponson lifted up to align with the bolt holes on the body of the tank. Not infrequently it proved impossible to re-align all the bolt holes perfectly and the holes had to be modified or re-bored. By the time the long process was completed, tempers were often short and not a few hands and fingers crushed. In hot weather, sweat ran off the men; in cold, fingers and hands turned blue.' (5)

A tank at Elveden prior to sponson-fitting. The sponsons arrived late and their absence led to some deformation of the hull structures, making the eventual fitting a very difficult job indeed.

It was at Elveden that the sponson re-attachment process was experienced at its very worst, for almost all of the tanks in the first batches arrived without them, sponson production having lagged slightly behind. The training schedule dictated that the tanks nevertheless be operated sponson-less, and the unwelcome discovery was made, when the sponsons did arrive, that in the course of training the hulls of some tanks had flexed and fractionally deformed, making sponson attachment a task of even more Herculean labour. (Later, as improved versions of the tank were introduced, the mountings were modified so that the sponsons could simply be slid inboard for rail or sea transport and slid out again after unloading, a labour-saving improvement for which all were devoutly grateful.)

Although many of the crewmen had previous mechanical experience, they obviously needed specialist support not only in respect of the wretched sponsons but for the multitude of other tricky tasks involved in maintaining and repairing the novel and complicated machines. For this purpose, temporary tank workshops were initially improvised in the open, but more permanent workshops were soon constructed as a matter of urgency.

Skilled engineering personnel to man the workshops came from a number of sources, but there was heavy reliance on the Army Service Corps and the area became home to a new specialised unit designated as No. 711 Motor Transport Company and mobilised specifically for duties at Elveden. This unit was commanded initially by Captain H.P.G. Steedman and then by Major Knopfe. The unit comprised ten officers and 303 other ranks, many of whom had previously worked in civilian workshops as fitters, turners and mechanics. They were equipped with general and specialist tool kits, lathes, drilling machines and the multiplicity of other items needed to make running repairs and to carry out the many minor modifications it was guessed were likely to be needed in the light of the training operations (as indeed proved to be the case). The quantity of support vehicles at the workshops' disposal demonstrated the incredibly rapid pace of mechanisation in an army which – like all others – had, until a few years' previously, possessed very few motor vehicles indeed: nine cars, thirteen vans, three buses, twenty-seven three-ton lorries, fifteen one-and-a half-ton lorries, seventeen motor-cycles and three 105h.p. Foster-Daimler tractors. The working days and nights of these A.S.C. men under Suffolk skies were long and arduous, for the tanks had been designed and built at great speed, and many were the adjustments and rectifications needed and many the breakdowns that had to be repaired.

SIX

Elveden: training and experiments

The initial difficulties described in the preceding chapter having been overcome, large-scale training commenced. This meant that everyone was quickly put to the test and, despite the general enthusiasm and high morale, some men inevitably turned out to be unsuitable: some suffered severe claustrophobia in the metal box that essentially constituted a tank, others quickly perceived the likelihood of a terrible death in a petrol-fuelled conflagration with slim hope of escape, and could not control their fear. Some simply found tanks too alien – motor-powered vehicles were still in their relative infancy – and preferred to take their chance as infantrymen. Others, in the time-honoured tradition of all armies everywhere, were 'duds' or slackers pushed out by their parent units. All of these were soon weeded-out, or weeded themselves out, and were sent back whence they came; but the total number of these was surprisingly small. The overwhelming majority remained and, said Lieutenant Basil Henriques, 'all felt a terrific pride in [their] Company and Section, and also as a tank crew against other tank crews. There was always healthy competition, and this competition carried us right out to France … Besides that, tank commanders had the very great advantage of training their crews themselves … We knew our men thoroughly'.(1) One of the benefits of the close harmony Henriques here emphasizes, which was much promoted by the physical proximity and shared dangers of incarceration in a giant metal box, was a welcome softening of the social barriers between officers and other ranks. There grew a greater regard by all concerned for what a man was and could do, rather than for his social standing. (While at Elveden, Henriques was still mourning the death of his elder brother, Ronald, a lieutenant in the Queen's Royal West Surrey Regiment who was killed in the Battle of the Marne only five weeks after the outbreak of war. The brothers came of a distinguished Anglo-Portuguese family and Basil was later to achieve prominence as a generous philanthropist and social reformer.)

One matter about which there was a lack of harmony was the boiler suits which had quite properly been issued to each man for day-to-day wear. These were viewed by all concerned – in the main, of course, ex-civilians, many of them used to wearing just such attire in 'Civvy Street' – as non-military and distinctly unsuitable for soldiers serving King and Country. Who wanted to face the enemy wearing a boiler suit? Or show a photo of such non-military 'splendour' to Mum and Dad? The men soon decided that in action in France they would wear their khaki uniforms in line with the rest of the army. (Of course, many clothes were temporarily discarded in the conditions of nigh-intolerable heat inside the vehicles and the boiler suits were re-donned out of the line when particularly mucky tasks had to be undertaken.)

Daily activity was always intense because, though the exact timetable for going into action was not foreseeable, everyone knew things would be very 'tight'. In fact, as we shall see, from the beginning of meaningful training by raw troops on a newly-invented weapon, to the day of their entry into battle was, at best, to be no more than three months and for some, significantly less.

A tank crew consisted of eight men: a lieutenant or second-lieutenant in command, a driver and two gearsmen, and four gunners. The first task was to introduce them to their tanks. Captain Richard Haigh (whose training took place later in the war) summed up what must have been the feelings of his predecessors at Elveden when they inspected a tank's white-painted interior for the first time: 'We looked round the chamber with eager curiosity. Our first thought was that seven men and one officer could never work in such a place ...' (2)

Even getting into or out of the tank was tricky: the C and D Company men found that entry to Female tanks was through small metal doors (one on each side) just large enough for a man to scramble through. Access was rather better in the Males, with a fairly large door in the rear of each sponson. Once inside either version, they discerned a space largely filled by machinery and weapons. In what remained, storage had to be found for iron rations, bread, tins of food, cheese, tea, sugar and milk, spare drums of engine oil and gear oil, drums of grease, water cans, approximately 300 shells plus copious quantities of machine-gun ammunition in the Males, 33,000 rounds of machine-gun ammunition in the Females, two boxes of revolver ammunition,

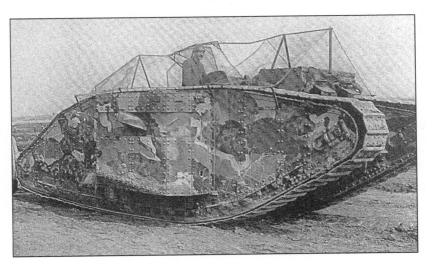

A tank – a 'Male' – at Elveden complete with anti-grenade netting. Note the crewman wearing the unpopular leather helmet.

five spare machine-gun barrels, wire cutters, carrier pigeons, a signalling set, personal kit, first aid boxes and numerous other items.

Headroom was no more than five feet and it was hardly possible to move round, let alone stand upright. Banging parts of the anatomy against unyielding metal was routine. To protect heads, leather helmets were issued but as these added to the intense heat, crews often discarded them and took the risk of a dented skull. (When helmets *were* worn, removing them before exiting the tank anywhere near a battle zone was later found to be prudent, as they were so shaped that even from a short distance they could easily be mistaken for the standard German 'coal-scuttle' helmet, with possible fatal consequences.) Obviously, things were particularly trying for big men: Basil Henriques found things very difficult at 6 feet 3 inches and one

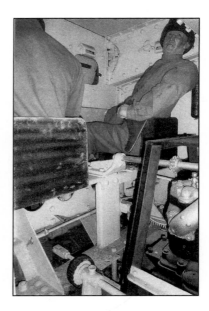

The commander's and driver's seating positions just ahead of the massive engine with the fuel tank dangerously positioned overhead.

A crew member just aft of the engine. A basket to hold carrier pigeons by his right hand and one of the many storage places for shells – the round tubes above his shoulder – should be noted.

officer, an exceptional 6 feet 7 inches, had to be returned to his unit simply through his physical inability to operate effectively. Worse than banging and bruising, though, was to burn oneself against the largely unshielded and blisteringly hot engine. This and its attendant gear mechanisms took up most of the space for the length of the tank, leaving a gangway of little more than a foot wide on either side.

Another piece of personal equipment trainees disliked was the face mask they were issued with. This was intended to give protection from 'bullet splash'. Bullet splash was caused by machine-gun and rifle fire striking the exterior of a tank, thus causing white-hot fragments of metal from the interior walls to detach themselves and fly off at high velocity. (Albert Driver - appropriately named - who drove a tank at the Battle of Cambrai said, 'Talk about noise, the sound of bullets on our plating was like fifty hailstorms on one corrugated iron shed'.) (3) The masks comprised a leather-covered solid metal plate around the upper

The leather helmet and face-mask, the latter to guard against 'bullet-splash', make a fearful combination.

part of the face, with slits in the eye area to permit vision, and a chain-mail 'beard' hanging down over the mouth and chin, which, in combination with the helmets, imparted wearers with the appearance of menacing mediæval warriors. The mask was, however, heavy and uncomfortable and was not often used. Consequently, tank crew members soon became recognisable by the pitted burn-marks on their faces and other areas of exposed skin.

At the front of the tank were two seats, one on the left for the commander (a junior officer), the one on the right for the driver. These two men's forward vision when not in action was adequate, as each had a reasonably large flap in front of him which he could open. However, when in action, these flaps necessarily had to be closed for protection and the view of the world was then severely limited, being either through the peephole or via the periscope with which each was provided. The 'peepholes in the armoured skin [were] mere slits framing prisms' and the periscopes afforded only a 'green, dim, misty view'. (4)

Corporal Parker (he who had been 'kidnapped' en route to the Somme) was soon established as a driving instructor along with a cadre of other experienced men with caterpillar-track backgrounds (in the case of Parker, mainly on Holt tractors). Parker recalled: 'We used to give ... the preliminary training to the officers. The officers would come over [to the Army Service Corps zone] and learn first with some of the men, senior ranks mostly, and then they'd borrow tanks from us to carry on with and teach their own junior men.'

All training had, of course, to commence with the ritual of engine-starting. Members of the crew would first be taught how to 'trip the mag' (the magneto, a device for supplying electricity to the sparking plugs) and then how to 'tickle the carburettor', in other words hand-prime it with an initial supply of petrol. This done, four of them would heave at a large starting handle at the rear of the engine and, with luck, the engine would burst into life with a great roar and a cloud of exhaust fumes. On the not-infrequent occasions that several 'goes' were needed, in cold or damp weather particularly, some crews resorted to injecting hot petrol direct into the cylinders by an unapproved and hazardous method involving a tin can and an old Lewis-gun magazine. Starting was not helped by the fact that the petrol in day-to-day-use was a mere 45 octane, significantly less than half the octane rating supplied for use in cars today. (Later, when battle loomed, the engines were treated to the more luxurious and effective aviation spirit.) Once operating, the engine consumed fuel, of whatever grade, at the voracious rate of half a mile per gallon and engine oil at the rate of four gallons a day.

Once the starting ritual was mastered, the next tricky task for the driver was to control the clutch. Drivers of modern cars fitted with manual gearboxes, accustomed as they are to light and easy clutch operation, can have little concept of the strength and judgement needed to operate the brutal mechanism on these 30-ton vehicles of nearly 100 years ago. Stalling was all too easy and re-starting was not a question of simply flicking a switch; as we have seen, four men were needed to swing the starting handle to bring the engine back to life. Patience was usually shown by other crew members during a trainee's first efforts but more than a handful of failures resulted in his receiving jeers and a hearty cursing from all concerned. He was, of course, able to criticise in kind when other crew members received their basic driver-training (so that someone else could take over if he, as main driver, were to be killed or wounded).

Steering ('swinging' in the tank jargon of the day) could be accomplished in a number of ways. The Mark One came equipped with a pair of ungainly tail wheels designed to act like a rudder on a ship and which, it was intended, would enable it to follow a curving course of 60 feet radius. In practice, the tails worked poorly and gave perpetual mechanical trouble. Fortunately, they were found to be largely unnecessary and were removed from all tanks shortly after the first experiences of battle.

The contemporary War Office publication, *The Tank Driver's Handbook,* describes the main methods of steering. For a slight turn, the commander could apply either the left or right track brake, thus slowing down one track. For 'turning quickly', the differential could be unlocked, and a high gear ratio engaged for one track and a low one for the other. However, both of these methods placed unwelcome strain on certain of the mechanical parts.(5)

Consequently, the preferred method was a third one, even though half the crew had to be involved in it. One man remembered: 'It was a hard job to turn [and] it needed four of [us] to work the levers and [we] took [our] orders by signals'. To turn right, first the tank had to stop. A knock on the right side by the tank commander would attract the attention of the right-hand operator. The driver would then raise a hand and make a clenched fist, the signal to put the right track into neutral. He then repeated the signal to show that this had been done. 'The officer, who controlled [the] two brake levers, would pull on the right one, which held the right track. The driver would accelerate and the tank would slew round on the stationary right track while the left track went into motion. As soon as the tank had turned sufficiently, the procedure was reversed.' (6) A similar process was involved in turning left. This steering procedure, cumbersome as it was, required many days of practice and co-ordination before attention could be turned to the crew's other tasks.

Crews soon encountered the problems of 'bellying' and 'ditching'. A tank 'bellied' if its underbody became stuck on a projection (a large tree stump sticking out of the ground, for example, or a peaked ridge too solid to be deformed by the tank's weight) so that its tracks could not grip the ground and simply spun uselessly. 'Ditching' occurred when the sides of a large shell-hole, crater, or trench, gave way under the weight of a tank manoeuvring near to it and the tank became stuck in the depression.

Generally, the Mark One's climbing ability was reckoned to be amazing and it could pull itself up out of deep trenches and haul itself up very steep and high banks. However, it could be defeated if the driver, juggling with throttle and clutch, failed to apply sufficient power or attempted the climb with inadequate momentum. This resulted in stalling. Even if it were possible to restart the engine (and frequently it was not, because the men assigned to use the starting handle could not find a footing on the heavily-sloping floor) the power of the engine was often insufficient to pull the tank up the slope from a standing start. Its own engine power would then have to be supplemented by another tank or a Holt tractor acting as a towing vehicle. Training drivers in the delicate skills needed to avoid their tank becoming trapped in this way included having to drive a tank up a steep, peaked ramp (or 'jump' as it came to be known) and then balancing it on its centre of gravity at the apex. (This is a trick still popular at public demonstrations of tank-driving skills today.) On one occasion in the earliest days at Elveden, when Robert Parker was driving Little Willie to demonstrate the trick to pupils, a ramp, made of tree trunks in this instance, collapsed and Little Willie's underplating was damaged in the tumble. However, Little Willie was soon restored to health in the A.S.C. workshop, for whose level of competence Parker developed a high regard.

Wire-crushing by the tanks' massive weight was much practised and was later supplemented by the use of towed grapnels to actually pull the wire out of the way.

As to the all-important gunners, they perched on motor cycle-like saddles in the sponsons, but adopted a kneeling position on the floor when aiming and firing their weapons. For the Males' six-pounder gunners, firing practice was initially hindered by the lack of stop butts for shells, which were essential if shell explosions through 'over-shoots' into neighbouring civilian areas were to be avoided, large though the training area was. Permission was therefore obtained from the War Office to fire on farm buildings but no sooner had this permission been granted then it was withdrawn by a War Office administrator fussily worried about damage to Lord Iveagh's private property. The embargo was only lifted after it was pointed out to whichever bureaucrat was responsible that this meant that the crews would have to go to war in France without ever having fired their weapons from their tanks. But, as Swinton ruefully recorded, valuable time was lost. (What was probably a specially-designed stop-butt, possibly only for use by machine-

Much of the troop accommodation consisted of tented camps. This is a small part of the largest of them at West Stow.

Part of the trench system. About 200 sandbags are visible in the foreground. It is sobering to consider that over a million were used in all, a testimony to the vast scale of the enterprise.

guns, was also constructed at some stage, though it has not been possible to determine exactly when. However, its remains can still be seen, nearly 100 years later.)

The firing practice problem having been resolved, the gunners got to work with a will. In the sponsons each 6-pounder gunner knelt on the floor with, as Captain Frank Mitchell recorded, 'his eye glued to the telescopic sight, his finger on the trigger … As the gun flashed vividly, a terrific booming sound filled the tank interior', loud enough to be heard in Thetford, 'and the breech recoiled past the gunner's face, which was protected by a shield. His mate, crouched on the narrow floor, quickly unloaded and thrust another shell into the breech. The empty shell cases fell on the floor and were thrown outside through a small opening on the underside of the sponson door … At times the trigger was pulled and no explosion resulted. Anxiously one waited a long minute of suspense, fearing that at any second the shell might explode in the breech. Then, gingerly opening the breech, the tank commander seized the offending shell and taking it boldly in his arms, flung it quickly through the opening at the bottom of the sponson door. Luckily, this was a rare occurrence'.

The operation of the 6-pounders was generally found to be considerably simpler than the equivalent tasks in respect of the machine-guns, and the 6-pounders could readily be swivelled in the direction of the selected targets. However, precise alignment as the tank roared and tumbled over rough ground was very difficult and it was found necessary to halt to achieve a high degree of accuracy, thus making the tank itself an easier target. In battle conditions, the Elveden 6-pounder men were to find that it was best to hold fire until no more than about 100 yards from the enemy, though bombarding fixed positions was found practicable up to 400 metres away. Machine-gun fire could be more readily 'sprayed' but ammunition was consumed rapidly and replacing the magazines was a deft and demanding operation.

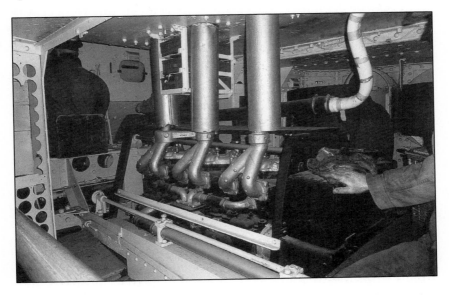

The 16-litre, 6-cylinder Daimler-Knight engine that occupied the bulk of the interior and generated near-intolerable heat and noise.

Other training tasks were many, including tactics, maintaining the six-pounders and machine-guns, signalling, mechanical knowledge, map-reading and navigation, first-aid skills, and co-ordination with infantry and other tanks. Revolver practice also featured, as crew members were issued with these rather than rifles as personal weapons. (On occasions these were to prove very useful when tanks came under close infantry attack, especially when crews had to bail out after a shell-strike or ditching.) Paramount, as Lieutenant Clough Williams-Ellis found, was the necessity to train crews together as a team, working under their officer, each member with his specialisation as brakeman, gearsman, driver or gunner, 'but each still part of an organic whole'. Crucially, too, each man had to train not only in his own speciality but in the rudiments of others' skills too, to enable him to take over from comrades in the event of casualties. Especially important in this respect was driving and much time and effort was spent in ensuring each man had sufficient experience to do this in an emergency.

Captain Groves, whom we met earlier, soon found himself to be a keen tankman: 'Being strong in those days I used to start up my tank with its 105 horsepower engine and do extra driving in the evenings'. His reference to 'being strong' emphasises the huge physical demands placed on tank crews by the extreme conditions in the tank's interior. Physical and mental acclimatisation to this was a major consideration. Even in training conditions, crew members had to tolerate the almost intolerable: noise was deafening and ventilation inadequate, so that the atmosphere became contaminated by poisonous carbon monoxide plus fuel and oil vapour from the engine and cordite fumes from the weapons. The noise meant that all orders and acknowledgements had to be given by signal. In relation to noise, crews were more than a little amazed, even allowing for the exigencies of the time, to find their tanks' engines were not fitted with silencers. Consequently, noise, sparks and even flames emerged spectacularly from the open exhaust pipes. Major J.F.C. Fuller, who after the war was to establish himself as a pre-eminent tank warfare strategist, recorded that 'many ingenious crews fitted to their machines crude types of silencers made out of oil drums, or adopted the plan of damping out the sparks by using wet sacks in relays, or covering the exhaust pipe in clay and mud'.(7) (This glaring defect was put right by fitting proper silencers at the factory as soon as time and circumstances permitted.)

Heat inside the tanks was overwhelming; even on a cold

Suffolk day temperatures could reach over 50 degrees centigrade (125 degrees Fahrenheit). Nor were the vehicles fitted with any form of springing, so that every jolt and bump, some of them massive, threw the men around like peas in a tin can. Most of these less-than-ideal characteristics had either been foreseen at the design stage or were soon experienced in testing, but the limited technologies of the day and the pressure for speed of design and simplicity of production meant they had to be accepted. The consequence was that, tough though things were at Elveden, prolonged exposure in battle conditions was sometimes to render crew members mentally confused. Not infrequently men lost consciousness inside the tank or collapsed when they emerged into fresh air.

A partial antidote to carbon monoxide was to eat bread, which to some degree absorbed carbon monoxide accumulated in the stomach, and so each tank crew was issued with a generous supply of loaves. (The severity of the problem – which, of course, the men first encountered at Elveden, though not in its most extreme forms – is illustrated by a report drawn up by the Royal Army Medical Corps later in the war, which recorded that after several hours' exposure to carbon monoxide, irrespective of bread consumption, 'the men [sometimes] sit and stare in front of them and merely repeat orders without putting them into execution. There is drowsiness and an irresistible desire to sleep. Two cases have occurred of defiance of discipline where superior officers have been attacked. In another, a man ran about shouting and cursing in an aimless manner'. In one instance, on a very long approach ride to the battlefront, 'the driver became totally unconscious and was found gripping his controls in a convulsive grip'. He was succeeded by the second driver and then by the tank commander, who both shared the same fate.)

In hindsight, it is amazing not that some men succumbed to the appalling environment but that the vast majority were able to carry out their duties at all, let alone with the efficiency and determination for which they became noted.

Overall, however, notwithstanding the huge amount of effort put into acclimatising the men to the conditions, and despite the thought and ingenuity put into the training process, there remained significant deficiencies in preparation for actual battle.

Additionally, it is clear that through shortage of time, and other pressures, the training regime was uneven, in that some crews missed out on important aspects of training from which others benefited. For example, Lieutenant Henriques observed later that, in the case of himself and his crew, 'we had no training with the infantry, even at home, and the infantry with whom we were to fight had never heard of us until they actually saw us in battle'. In his case, 'we had never driven in England with our [tank] flaps closed so that we had never used the periscope and had only driven with a clear view'.

Additionally, from time to time crews had to be diverted from their training routines to participate in battlefield experiments, notably in respect of communications and route guidance. As to communications, Swinton recorded: 'It seemed quite possible that one or two machines, being bullet-proof, might in an attack penetrate far ahead of the infantry and be in a position to gather information of the utmost value not obtainable from the air. The obvious way was to arrange for passing this back by wireless' and after experiments at Elveden and back in the works at Lincoln, the Royal Engineer Experimental Wireless Establishment did succeed in producing a small spark-transmission set with a range of about three miles. It employed a short, folding, steel mast and was designed to fit into the very cramped space available. Sadly, however, its use proved entirely impracticable owing to the noise and vibration within the tanks when their engines were running. Other expedients therefore had to be resorted to.

Swinton again: 'A secondary method of communicating back, namely by aeroplane, was concurrently evolved . . . the RFC [from Snarehill] handing over to us a large number of special daylight signalling lamps for communication between tanks and aeroplanes'. Unfortunately, it soon became obvious that the chain of transmission from tank to aeroplane to airfield and then back out to relevant commanders would, in battlefield conditions, be so cumbersome and slow as to be almost useless. 'Experiments were made in laying telephone cable by a tank. A groove in the ground, some six inches deep, was cut by a ploughshare fixed at the back of the machine, and into this the cable was paid out from a drum. No conclusive results were achieved, and the short length of cable that could be carried on a tank did not warrant great hope of success', especially as wire, unless buried very deeply, was acutely vulnerable to disruption by enemy shellfire.

Despite these praiseworthy and ingenious efforts to provide a scientific solution, the technology of the day was not quite up to the task, and this was a great handicap. Science thus having failed, Nature had to be employed, and so it came about that carrier pigeons were experimented with for reporting back. They came to be frequently used in action, and were generally found to be very successful. Naturally, there was a delay whilst they flew back to their reporting centre and, of course, a limitation was that they could operate only *from* the tanks and not take messages *to* them. Four birds, kept in a basket, were allocated to each tank. One man in each crew was selected as their handler; he was trained to care for and feed them, told how to fix a message capsule onto a leg, and how to launch the bird from the tank. No pigeon has left a record of how it felt about the appalling conditions inside the tanks, but some men reckoned to have observed a look of relief on the pigeons' faces as they were released into the fresh (if bullet-torn) air.

We must have great sympathy with Swinton and his people in relation to these communication difficulties: quite simply, the absence of compact, reliable, two-way communications equipment was a massive handicap at all levels of command throughout the war. It is ironic that the rapid development of so much other technology made the absence of this one extremely acute; this fact should on no occasion be overlooked when making judgements about First World War commanders, strategy and tactics.

However, the Elveden experiments did give rise to the creation of a very basic method of short-range communication between tank and tank, comprising metal discs and small flags waved out of the manhole in the roof. 'It was realised,' says Swinton, 'that the discs might be shot away and would probably be invisible in the dusk and smoke of battle, and that only the simplest messages could be signalled. Inefficient as this system was, it was all that was possible'.

As to route guidance and way-finding, the vision available to tank commanders and drivers was very limited and this 'made it extremely difficult to steer and maintain direction over a long distance by reference only to what they could see immediately around them'.

In an endeavour to ameliorate the problem, compasses were resorted to. Gunner Robert Tate, from Sunderland and the eldest of seven children, was one of the earliest of the Elveden men to undertake compass-guided cross-country runs over the Suffolk landscape, including some at night, using Little Willie.

Swinton states that the compasses were of a special 'de-magnetised' type, de-magnetisation being necessary to obviate distortions triggered by the mass of the tanks' metal hulls. This is puzzling, as it is difficult to see how a compass stripped of its (literally) guiding principle could work at all. It is possible that the compasses in question were, in fact, gyro-compasses, which had been invented by the American, Elmer Sperry, in 1911. In any event, whatever their nature, re-conditioned compasses were obtained from the Admiralty Compass Department and a naval instructor seconded to Elveden to train crews in their use. However, in practice, they were never to prove of more than limited assistance.

As a possible secondary means of assisting the drivers, Swinton ordered a supply of twenty tethered balloons which it was envisaged would be flown behind the British lines at a height of about a thousand feet, on which crews could look back and obtain visual bearings or take compass readings. Again, this system was found wanting and not used in action, though crews did find that they were occasionally able to get some rough help from obtaining bearings on British and German tethered observation balloons. (There is today a farm known as Balloon Barn Farm near the southern boundary of the area, and it may be thought that here were stored Swinton's balloons; in fact, it housed a small airship used during army manoeuvres in East Anglia in 1912.)

Much thought was given to camouflaging the tanks to render them less conspicuous on the battlefield. The principal figure in this connection was the prominent artist, Solomon J. Solomon, a member of the Royal Academy and for the duration of the war a Royal Engineer with the rank of Lieutenant-Colonel. Solomon's wartime speciality was camouflage and in the spring and summer of 1916 his main task was to devise a suitable treatment for the new machines. At Elveden, in keeping with his perceived eccentricity in the eyes of fellow officers and men, his personal transport was a pony – this in a unit which, of all those in the army, was the least equine-minded.

Solomon had already been to France to study the type of countryside in which it was thought the tanks would fight. His conclusions reached, he set about personally painting Mother in a barn at Bernersfield Farm as if, according to Basil Henriques, he was covering a canvas for the Royal Academy. Henriques thought the result was 'a kind of jolly landscape in green against a pink sunset sky'. Once Solomon had finished his prototype, each tank crew was issued with gallons of suitable paints and copied Solomon's design as best they could onto their own vehicle. Few of the soldiers would previously have believed they would ever find themselves emulating the work of an eminent artist. Unfortunately, it was soon found in France that Solomon's design was in practice less than satisfactory, and the tanks were quickly re-painted in what became their characteristic muddy brown. Possibly Solomon's artistic eye had been too much drawn to that part of the delightful French countryside not yet despoiled by the mud and dereliction of battle.

Thus it was that life at Elveden comprised constant training, instruction and practice; but, at the end of every day, however weary the men were, yet another unpopular and lengthy task had to be undertaken – the greasing of the tanks' tracks and runners. Captain Mitchell recorded: 'The tank is a monster with a voracious appetite, and besides devouring huge quantities of petrol, has to be fed daily on grease. This was injected by means of grease guns and, as many apertures for greasing the tracks and rollers were placed at the base of the tank, it was necessary to lie flat on the ground to perform this sticky rite. When the ground was muddy, the language of the grease-gun brigade must have made the ears of the tank inventors tingle furiously'.

Nor did the roar of tank engines at Elveden subside at night, for crews had to practice approaches across country in the dark to get to the forming-up points behind the lines, as they would have to do in France. This was difficult, says Swinton, as the compasses never proved wholly reliable, 'but the task of the drivers was [now] much facilitated by the route for each machine being marked out on the ground with tape dipped in luminous paint. Moving in single file was assisted by the tail lamp at the back of each machine'.

Swinton was himself impressed by his nocturnal experience of the machines he commanded: 'For the first time to feel the night air quiver with the throbbing of the engines and then to see the sinister shapeless masses loom up and lurch off into the darkness was an uncanny experience not easily forgotten'. (In AD63, on much the same spot, and with feelings similar to Swinton's, Queen Boudicca of the Iceni tribe, which had a major gathering centre nearby, may have watched her horse-drawn war chariots, which in her famous Revolt were to intimidate the Romans just as Swinton's motor-driven tanks were to intimidate the Germans more than 1,800 years later.)

SEVEN

Rest and Relaxation (though not very much)

The weeks and months of stressful physical and mental exercise on the part of everyone at Elveden had to be balanced by occasional relaxation, however brief. Thus, the long days and nights of training were occasionally broken by trips by lorry to Bury St Edmunds, where officers would dine at the Angel Hotel and the NCOs at the less grand Suffolk Hotel.

Immediately adjoining the Suffolk Hotel (now Waterstone's bookshop and the Edinburgh Woollen Mill) was a series of blown-apart shops, a grim reminder to the Elveden men of the existence of an enemy weapon as new as their own – the

Trips were sometimes possible to Thetford or Bury St Edmunds. The favourite drinking establishment of other ranks was the Suffolk Hotel (at right) notwithstanding the adjacent damage caused by a Zeppelin raid in April 1915.

Zeppelin. The shops had been set ablaze in an attack by a Zeppelin on 30th April 1915 when it had flown over Moyses Hall, down the Buttermarket and circled over Abbey Gardens.

In all, it dropped more than fifty high-explosive and incendiary bombs here, elsewhere in the town and in the surrounding villages. Happily, no living being was killed, except an unfortunate collie dog. (A further raid on the town on 31st March 1916, in the Elveden training ground's early days, unfortunately resulted in six fatalities.)

Generally, the rank and file soldiers were not so lucky as the officers and NCOs in participating in such trips: one recalled that 'being so far from a town rather spoiled our spare time, unless one possessed a motor bicycle for a run into Thetford'. (1) However, various facilities were provided on site. There was a large recreational marquee put up by the Young Men's Christian Association (the YMCA). The *Bury Free Press*, which had access to the non-secret areas and, of course, absolutely no knowledge of what they contained, reported on August 16th that 'Refreshments are provided and there are the usual postal facilities, reading, writing and games tables ... Concerts and entertainments are arranged at intervals ...'

The men, when time allowed, occasionally put on a concert party themselves. Two of the principal participants were Acting Corporal Frank Vyvyan and 2nd Lieutenant Eric Purdy, both of whom were to become regular performers in 'The Willies', the unofficial entertainment group set up after the move to France. Vyvyan, who was to be awarded the Military Medal and the Distinguished Conduct Medal, was the son of actor Herbert Vyvyan and his wife Alice. Purdy, a popular officer later to be seriously wounded, often played the part of a curate.

The YMCA did not fail to take advantage of the opportunity to supplement the official Army church parades and

As might be expected, officers on an excursion to Bury St Edmunds preferred the more up-market, and more expensive, Angel Hotel.

from the outset incorporated evening prayers and Sunday afternoon services into their recreational programme. Whether these reminders of the divine were popular is questionable: one of the troops favourite songs, sung, ironically, to the tune of 'What a Friend We Have in Jesus', heralded the pleasure they would feel post-war in having 'no more Church Parades on Sundays'. (That German troops, every one of whom had 'Gott mit uns' – 'God with us' – engraved on his belt buckle were being simultaneously urged to pray to the same god for *their* succour and success is an irony that, as in wars before and since, seems to have struck neither the YMCA nor the Churches in general.)

The *Bury Free Press* also reported on another concert party, held in August, at which wounded and limbless soldiers from Elveden Convalescent Hospital were present. These damaged men must have given rise to sober thoughts in the troops of the Heavy Section as they readied themselves for battle.

As well as the official facilities, small informal canteens were set up by the troops themselves, again with newspapers and magazines and in one or two cases a piano. Robert Parker, by now a sergeant, could still remember in the 1970s how he and some of his fellow sergeant-instructors provided a makeshift mess for themselves: '... there were seven of us in [this particular] sergeants' mess and we had a Willie cover – a tank cover – strung up on a long line between two trees, and a six-foot barrack room table and two six-foot forms [benches] and that's where we lived and died'.

These Army Service corps sergeants, like others of all ranks, benefited from one universally welcomed feature of Elveden, that Army rations could be readily supplemented by the pheasants and rabbits which abounded in the district. This was very much to the good, for it seems that the Army supply chain was never as generous or proficient as it might have been in getting adequate food supplies through. Cooking, both of official supplies and of unofficial supplements, was eased by the existence of a useful ledge on the tank engine which could be employed for frying bacon, bread, and corned beef ('bully beef' or 'bully', as it was called, and comprising rather more fat than lean). Other staples were Machonocies' meat and vegetable soup (reportedly much more veg than meat) and Tickler's jam. The latter came in two varieties, plum and apple or apricot; most reckoned that they could detect no difference of flavour between the two. But what the troops 'ran' on, just as much as the tanks ran on petrol, was British Army tea: very hot, very strong, very sweet and preferably made with condensed milk. Many crews kept a supply of hot water to hand by means of a billy-can strapped to their tank's exhaust pipe.

For those inclined, there was swimming in the River Lark or bracing runs across the heathland. But, as is eternally the case, the greatest pleasure and relaxation came from receiving letters and parcels from home, family and friends.

Swimming in the River Lark was no doubt hugely welcome after a day spent in a tank.

EIGHT
Very Important Persons

From time to time, naturally still preserving the strictest secrecy, Elveden attracted some exotic visitors, leading to interruptions in the daily routine. The Chief of the Imperial General Staff (C.I.G.S.), General Sir William Robertson, arrived on the 20th July for an inspection and demonstration to be held the following day. Robertson is remarkable for the fact that he was, and remains, the only man in the history of the British Army to rise from the rank of private to Field Marshall. To have done this in the Victorian and Edwardian eras, with their acute conscious-ness of class, was doubly astounding, particularly as Robertson was never able (indeed, did not even try) to rid himself of the habit of dropping his aitches. ' 'Orace, you're for 'Ome' he once famously said when stripping a general of his command.

Robertson was accompanied by several other senior officers and, from the Government itself, Mr David Lloyd George, at that point Secretary of State for War and Minister of Munitions and later to become Prime Minister. These V.I.P.s, plus Swinton and his most important aides (including the Heavy Section's Liaison Officer with Army HQ in France, Lieutenant- Colonel Brough), spent the night of the 20th at Elveden Hall as guests of Lord Iveagh. On learning that Lord Iveagh had still not been made aware of what was happening so mysteriously on his own land, Robertson decided that at last Iveagh should be told, though on a pledge of honour that he would not divulge his new knowledge to anyone.

Accordingly, after dinner, the seven most senior members of the group adjourned to Elveden Hall's billiard room. This was very large and in consequence of Duleep Singh's redecoration of the Hall during his time there, Eastern in appearance. It was almost in gloom, said Swinton, except 'for the fierce glare poured downwards from the billiard table lamps in their green shades'. Bent over the table, studying a large map unrolled by General Maurice, the Director of Military Operations, were the two figures in evening dress and the five in khaki. Maurice explained what it was planned the tanks would do to help in the Somme offensive. He emphasised the terrible effects of the German machine-gun fire and explained how it was hoped that, in the shape of the tank, a counter-weapon had been devised.

Before going to sleep, Swinton lay in bed in his luxurious room in the Hall, thinking about the fact that 'hard by, in the silent darkness, all among the young partridges, lay crouched our dragons [tanks], fed, groomed and anointed in readiness for their dress-rehearsal on the morrow. And farther off, 150 miles away, amidst the roar of artillery and the fitful stutter of machine guns, intermittently lit up [by flares] lay the real stage – the blood-drenched battlefield on the Somme'.

The following morning the party assembled at the viewing stand and witnessed a major 'battle' in which 25 tanks, supported by British infantry and opposed by 'German' infantry, assaulted the enemy lines. Within an hour-and-a-half of the operation he had witnessed, Lloyd George was handed aerial photographs of it, snapped, landed, developed, printed and sent over to Elveden by the Royal Flying Corps at Snareshill. The unit involved was probably 35 Squadron which had been formed at Thetford as an Army co-operation squadron in February. (The other squadron there at the time was No. 51, which was trained for anti-Zeppelin patrols.) Sadly, no copy of the photographs is now known to exist.

We have seen that Lloyd George had been impressed when

The rough-hewn reviewing stand used by VIPs, including the King, to observe the world's first tank force preparing for war.

witnessing the demonstration by the single tank at Hatfield earlier in the year. He was even more impressed by the spectacle of twenty-five of them simultaneously roaring and wallowing and climbing and shooting their way across the smoking and exploding Elveden 'battlefield'.

Lloyd George also recorded the first example of successful resistance to a tank attack when, at the end of the demonstration, he followed the trail left by one of the 'elephantine monstrosities when it crashed through shrubberies, smashing young trees and bushes into the earth, and leaving behind it a wide trail of destruction ... in the middle of it I found a partridge's nest full of eggs - and incredible to relate, not a single egg had been broken!'

Five days later, on the 26th July, officers and men were given a few hours warning that a Russian general was arriving. In fact, the 'Russian general' was King George V accompanied by a small entourage. The royal party came by special train to Barnham station. Once the King had stepped onto the reviewing stand overlooking the demonstration area, the cover story was of course exploded and the news of the royal arrival spread round the camp like wildfire. The demonstration was a much smaller one than that of the previous week (just five tanks and no 'enemy') but the King's experience was much enlivened by being taken for a run in a tank himself. The driver selected for this high-prestige task was Gunner Robert Tate who, as we have seen, had been the driver for many of the cross-country experiments and who must have been very good at his job indeed. Tate was amused by the way the King's royal person was thrown around like an ordinary mortal's as he drove him across some especially bumpy ground. History does not record whether or not Tate selected the terrain with mischief aforethought. After all was over and the King prepared to depart, the monarch was surrounded by cheering troops as he drove away.

The men were beginning to realise just how important they and their new 'toys' were . . .

NINE

A Difference of Opinion

As June moved towards its junction with July, there came to a head a fundamental difference of opinion about tank strategy. Involved, on the one hand, were Swinton and other officers in charge at an operational level and, on the other, the decision-makers in British High Command.

In a report prepared in February 1916 ('Notes on the Employment of Tanks') Swinton had encapsulated the view of himself and all the senior tank pioneers: 'Since the chance of success of an attack by tanks lies almost entirely in its novelty and in the element of surprise, it is obvious that no repetition of it will have the same opportunity of succeeding as the first unexpected effort. It follows therefore that these machines should not be used in driblets (for instance, as they may be produced) but that the fact of their existence should be kept as secret as possible *until the whole are ready to be launched, together with an infantry assault, in one great combined operation.*' (Author's emphasis.) (1)

Much the same conclusion about avoiding premature first use was to be reached by Colonel Estienne, France's equivalent to Swinton. (The French had picked up the idea of tanks, but that nation's tank development was lagging a long way behind Britain's.) Indeed, four or five months after Swinton's paper, Estienne was to make a personal appeal to the British to hold back. Was Estienne calling for delay until the French were ready with their tanks too? If so, it is fair to say it would have been very unwise for the British to have held back on that ground alone, for the first French tanks proved to be failures; their first attack was not to take place until April 1917 and was disastrous. (However,

73

a year later, in April 1918, French engineering recovered its form and produced the very fine Renault FT-17 light tank; this was manufactured in larger numbers than any other Allied tank and was also the first to incorporate a revolving gun turret.)

However, whilst apparently recognising the strength of all this advice for prudent delay, the decision-makers in the British High Command rejected it. In fact, it was made clear to Swinton that there was a determination to employ tanks as soon as possible, even if only in very small numbers. In part, this was because the British Army found itself in circumstances of unprecedented difficulty, for while the tank crews at Elveden had been starting up their machines early on the morning of Sunday the 1st July, far away in France the British Army had embarked on by far the largest offensive in its entire history to date. This offensive, the Battle of the Somme, was launched neither at a time nor in a place the British themselves favoured, but under an urgent military and political requirement to relieve their French ally from the seemingly endless German attack at Verdun, the object of which was to bleed the French Army white. (The Germans nearly succeeded, but the French famously swore 'They Shall Not Pass' and, with enormous fortitude and at the cost of the most terrible casualties, held on.) Now, to compound the French and German bloodbath, the gloriously sunny opening day of the British offensive resulted in disaster: 19,240 men killed and 38,270 wounded. In a dreadful contrast to the weather, this was the blackest-ever day for the British Army, before or since.

Following this, the already-existing pressure on the men at Elveden to ready the tanks and crews for action doubled and re-doubled. The Somme offensive, now clearly recognised as likely to be a titanic struggle, seems to have given rise to a belief that any method of increasing its chance of success should be employed as soon as humanly possible, irrespective of any longer-term adverse consequences. Some of this sense of urgency emanated personally from the British commander-in-chief, Field Marshall Douglas Haig.

It is worth emphasising here that Haig – contrary to much popular belief and despite still being frequently caricatured as a blinkered and stupid cavalryman – was, though perhaps not more than averagely talented, emphatically *not* a fool. His populist and superficial critics seem to forget that it was this man, the man they decry, who in the last months of 1918 led the British Army to the greatest series of victories it has ever had, before or since. (In particular, Joan Littlewood's brilliant 'Oh, What a Lovely War', which many people believe accurately portrays the First World War, is grossly inaccurate in numerous fundamental respects. By way of example, Littlewood's vivid portrayal of the British generals as entirely remote and uncaring, leading claret-drinking lives in fine French chateaux whilst feeling no concern about, and little knowledge of, the conditions faced by their troops, is far from the truth. In fact, as the late Richard Holmes (probably the most respected military historian of recent times) pointed out, far from having no concept or concerns about front-line conditions, seventy-eight British generals were killed in action or died of wounds in the First World War - *more than four times the number killed in the Second*. In short, it can be confidently asserted that Joan Littlewood's military and historical talents were probably on a par with Douglas Haig's ability to direct a film or stage a musical.)

Certainly, Haig was always open to technological innovation and his enthusiasm for the tank was immediate. Indeed, he was later to widen the whole scope of military thinking by suggesting to the Royal Navy that it conduct experiments with special flat-bottomed boats for running tanks ashore on the

Belgian coast with a view to breaking through the German lines there. (The scheme never eventuated, but Haig's foresight foreshadowed many such operations in the Second World War, most conspicuously, of course, D-Day.)

Nevertheless, despite Haig's enthusiasm for the tanks, the subtleties of ensuring their successful introduction and modes of operation seem in significant measure to have escaped him. In short, it could be argued that by his immediate perception of the tank's importance he acquitted himself of the sin of Ludditism but committed the sin of premature use. In extenuation, it must be pleaded that he was a man operating under conditions of immense pressure of every kind. It can also be maintained that it was in fact wise to conduct an experimental attack on a small scale simply to gain operational experience. In any event, insistent demands for early use emanated from the highest levels; whether Swinton himself was sufficiently firm in withstanding the pressure, or whether it was simply not withstandable by an officer of his comparatively junior rank, we do not know. Nor can we totally rule out the possibility that in the end Swinton himself felt some temptation to see his new 'toys' in action.

The basic truth is probably to be found in what Albert Stern recorded about a meeting he had with Lloyd George, the Secretary of State for War, some time after the Somme's terrible opening day. He was informed then that, though the arguments for holding back were understood, the heavy casualties sustained and the lack of success in breaching the German lines might well lead to a lowering in the Army's morale; it was thought that the use of the new weapons might be one way of maintaining it. Lloyd George himself later said he had already seen Balfour and 'begged him' to intervene to prevent premature use. Though not disagreeing, Balfour had referred him to Sir William Robertson, the Chief of the Imperial General Staff. Lloyd George records: 'I urged [Robertson] to exert his influence with the Commander-in-Chief [Haig]. He answered in his most laconic style, "Haig wants them" ' (or more likely, as we saw earlier, " 'Aig wants 'em.") In short, times were bad and everything had to be tried as soon as possible.

There was a final point, too. In his report of February 1916, Swinton had said that not only should the tanks be employed first in devastating numbers, but that it was essential to deploy them *only* on the right kind of terrain – for example, avoiding areas with canals or rivers, deep railway cuttings with steep sides, woods and orchards, all of which would impede or halt progress. He foresaw the possibility that, used in sufficient quantities, tanks could break through the enemy's defensive zone in a single day and he therefore heavily emphasised the necessity for making foolproof arrangements for immediately sending forward reinforcements of every description – troops, guns, ammunition and supplies. Few of these points were to be fully understood and accepted by the Army as a whole during the tanks' first year of operations.

We should not leave our consideration of these disputes, and their effects on conscientious individuals, without recalling the fate of a man closely involved in them, Lieutenant Colonel John Brough. As recorded earlier, he had been sent to France as the Heavy Section's liaison officer with the 'powers that be' in the British Expeditionary Force and it seems that he fairly soon established for himself a reputation for being 'awkward'. This might simply have meant that he was vigorous in promoting the tank men's views, and thus categorised as insufficiently accom- modating to the wishes of those in high authority. In any event, arising from the long-term tensions brought about by his unenviable position, in July 1917, and with the clash of ideas still unresolved, the 43-year-old Brough was to walk up a quiet

French country lane and kill himself with a shot to the head from his Webley pistol. After the war, the Army Council formally declared that 'the strain of military duty undoubtedly caused the mental condition that prompted this officer's suicide'. (National Archives WO 339/59279) Thus his sad and desperate death was as much a consequence of the war as if he had met his end in a shell-hit tank.

These men were soon to be directly affected by the outcome of the high-level debates on tank strategy and tactics. The original caption read :

Some of the boys of the 'Landships'

Black Watch and Royal Defence Corps soldiers of the Guard Force.
Note the dog; army units almost always managed to acquire such a
follower.

Tank tracks, clearly demonstrating the ability to cope with very high
and steep obstacles.

TEN

Meanwhile, Back at Elveden ...

The festering differences of strategic opinion remained unknown at the level of the junior officers, NCOs and men at Elveden, which was no doubt fortunate for the maintenance of morale. But the pressure exerted to get the tanks into action with minimal delay meant that training had to be conducted at a ferocious pace. The consequence was that instructors often found themselves unable to ensure that every crew received the desired amount of tuition and practical experience, either in terms of depth or duration.

In a few cases, training was lacking to a disturbing degree. Clough Williams-Ellis in his book *The Tank Corps* quotes one unfortunate tank commander as later recalling that '... I and my crew did not have a tank of our own over the whole time we were in England ... as our tank went wrong the day it arrived ... we had no reconnaissance or map reading ... no practices and lectures on the compass ... and no practice in considering orders. This was a thing I very much missed when I got out to France. When you work with a Division you get very long orders, and you have to analyse these orders to discover what concerns you and what does not ...'

Nevertheless, as Williams-Ellis emphasised, even the defects in this unhappy case were ameliorated by the high quality of the crews, for 'the men were picked individuals of more than ordinary intelligence, and soon became extraordinarily keen on their work'. Basil Henriques summed things up similarly: 'We felt a terrific pride in our Company and Section, and also as a tank crew against other tank crews. There was always healthy competition, and this competition carried us right out to France.'

This enthusiasm meant that everything to do with the tanks, including day-to-day battlefield Do's and Don'ts, was much discussed not only in formal sessions but informally over meals, over a mug of 'char', or round the campfires at night. In August, Swinton finally felt able to put down in simple, aide-memoire form, a handy guide to the most important tactical points. His document, scrawled out on a single sheet of paper now archived in the Tank Museum at Bovington and simply titled *Tank Tips*, puts in a nutshell the lessons learned in training or presciently considered in the peaceful fields of Suffolk. His summary was to prove remarkably accurate in terms of actual battlefield experience:

- Remember your orders

- Shoot quick

- Shoot low. A miss which throws dust in the enemy's eyes is better than one which whistles in his ear

- Shoot cunning

- Shoot the enemy while they are rubbing their eyes

- Economise ammunition and don't kill a man three times

- Remember that trenches are curly and dugouts deep - look round the corners

- Watch the progress of the fight and your neighbouring tanks

- Watch your infantry whom you are helping

- Remember the position of your own line

- Smell out the enemy's machine guns and other small guns and kill them first with your 6-pounders

- You must ferret out where [the machine guns] are, judging by the following signs:

Sound

Dust

Smoke

A shadow in a parapet

A hole in a wall, haystack, rubbish heap, wood stack or pile of bricks

- Machine guns will usually be placed to fire slantways across the front and to shoot along the wire. One 6-pounder shell that hits the loophole of a machine gun emplacement will do it in.
- Use the 6-pounder with care; shoot to hit and not to make a noise
- Never have any gun, even when unloaded, pointing at your own infantry, or a 6-pounder gun pointed at another Tank.
- It is the unloaded gun that kills the fool's friends.
- Never mind the heat
- Never mind the noise
- Never mind the dust
- Think of your pals in the infantry
- Thank God you are bullet-proof and can help the infantry, who are not
- Have your masks always ready

Swinton's penultimate point about the tanks' being bullet-proof was deliberately ingenuous: death by burning, by scalding steam and water escaping from the cooling system,

82

death by asphyxiation or by lying inextricably trapped in tangled metal, any or all of which could ensue from a shell-strike, he carefully did not mention, obvious though these things were to all. No doubt Harry grinned wryly to Jack: ' 'E says there's nothing at all to worry about, mate. May as well cancel the insurance'.

ELEVEN

Preparing to leave for France

All in all, the tanks had been hard-used at Elveden. In mid-August, as departure for France loomed, Swinton and his senior officers grew increasingly concerned that the repairs and servicing needed to bring them back to a condition fit for action could not be completed from the resources available on site in the limited time left. But the ever-resourceful Albert Stern guaranteed to have all the tanks put in order within ten days. '... I went to Birmingham and asked for volunteers from the employees of the Metropolitan Wagon Company to get the tanks ready within a week to go to France. I told them that accommodation and food would be difficult to find, but without the slightest hesitation Mr. Wirrick ... and forty men started for Thetford. They were billeted by the Chief Constable. The difficulty was the food. The Army could not supply it. I therefore went to Colonel Thornton, General Manager of the Great Eastern Railway, and he immediately put a restaurant car on a siding at the camp and fed the men until the work was done. It took them less than ten days.'

The time had come for C and D companies to depart for France, whilst leaving A and B companies (which had arrived from Bisley a little later than C and D) to continue to work up at Elveden until they, too, were ready for their baptism of fire (which was to come on 14th November and is not dealt with in this account). The transfer of the C and D company men, their tanks and supporting equipment was assigned the code-name 'Operation Alpaca'. The first company to go was C: some thirty officers and 250 other ranks. On 13th August Swinton gathered them all together for the last time in peaceful Suffolk 'under the pine trees on a slight rise behind the centre of the [mock] British line' and gave them a fatherly talk, reminding them in particular of their duty to serve their entirely unprotected comrades in the infantry.

The two nights following the 13th were devoted to the onerous work of loading the first thirteen tanks and their detached sponsons onto the flat-bed railway wagons marshalled at the Culford Lodge siding, ready for despatch on the morning of the 16th. Tanks and sponsons alike were cocooned (as always) in tarpaulins to protect them from prying eyes during transit and were sent on their way to Avonmouth Docks at Bristol. They were escorted by Army Service Corps drivers who on arrival drove them off the flat-beds, positioned them for lifting on board the transport ships and manoeuvred them in the holds. These tanks crossed to France on 20th/21st August. The remaining thirteen tanks of the Company were similarly loaded in the ensuing few days and crossed the Channel on the 24th/25th. The officers and men went by train to Southampton and there embarked for Le Havre.

D Company's tanks, sponsons, ancillary equipment and stores commenced their transfer overseas on 25th August. First to depart was a train carrying thirteen tanks, which had been loaded up on the night of the 25th/26th and which moved off from the siding early in the morning. A second train, loaded up on the following night, carried the 26 sponsons for the tanks and all the spare guns, ammunition and stores for Nos.1 and 2 Sections. Ironically, many were loaded onto a former German vessel, the *Altair*, which had been requisitioned by the Admiralty on the outbreak of war and renamed the S.S. *Hunsgate*. (1)

The 155 officers and men of 1 & 2 Sections of D Company entrained at Thetford Bridge Station on Monday 28th August at

6 o'clock in the morning. On arrival at Liverpool Street they marched across London to Waterloo, then journeyed to Southampton to board the troopship *Caesarea* which sailed for Le Havre that evening. The officers and men of Nos. 3 and 4 Sections, 106 in number, left Thetford Bridge Station to join them shortly afterwards.

The dark-hours loadings involved in Operation Alpaca, though arduous, generally went well enough, but a little before midnight on 2nd/3rd September when the remaining thirteen tanks of 'D' Company (those belonging to Nos. 1 & 2 Sections) were being loaded, there was what Swinton, with typical understatement, describes as 'an exciting episode', namely a bombing raid by a German Zeppelin. These were giant lighter-than-air machines, 550 feet long, with crew, engines and bombs suspended in gondolas slung underneath. They appeared like ocean liners floating through the sky.

A Zeppelin similar to the one that raided Elveden; the brooding darkness of this poor quality photo seems to symbolise the threat posed to the people of Britain.

Swinton's account continues: 'In and out of the cold light and exaggerated shadows of the acetylene flares, the [tanks] were crawling, one by one, up the ramp, against which a train of flat trucks had been backed, and lurching along the train as far as each could go. Tanks were everywhere; sponsons were everywhere; and all around was a scene of bustle. Suddenly, a whistle shrilled out, the dazzling light changed to darkness, all the blacker by contrast, the din died down to silence and the vibrating air became still. Then a faint drone in the distance, the dull roar of bombs, and a Zeppelin was seen high up in the direction of Thetford. The airship came on and on, the roar of its engines growing ever louder'.

In fact, the Zeppelin flew directly over both the training area and Elveden Hall and was low enough for the gondolas under its vast, cigar-shaped body to be distinguished by the naked eye. There was an instant suspicion that the Germans had somehow discovered the tanks' existence and were intent on destroying them before they got to France. In fact, the Germans had no knowledge of tanks at all, though the Zeppelin in question (L32, commanded by Oberleutnant zur Zee Werner Peterson) was part of the biggest-ever Zeppelin raid on Britain, sixteen of them taking part. Peterson had already dropped incendiaries (to no effective purpose) just outside Thetford at Two Mile Bottom. If L32 was definitely seeking *something* in the area, it may have been the Royal Flying Corps airfield at Snarehill. In the event, after dropping a number of explosive bombs somewhat randomly, it flew away, much to the relief of all below but leaving a suspicion in their minds that the secret was 'out'. This suspicion was compounded when, about three hours later, a second Zeppelin, (L16 under the command of Kapitanleutnant Erich Sommerfeldt) dropped incendiaries at the village of West Stow, close to the Area's boundary, though once more to no effect.

The historic significance of this episode was that for the first time in history, the two factors which were largely to dominate warfare up to and including our own times, tanks and aerial bombing, had come into close proximity, though only the men on the ground knew it. For most of them, the sound of the bomb explosions was their first experience of being 'under fire', however ineffective and small in scale, before leaving for the fields of France or, in the case of what we shall dub 'the Palestine contingent', the Middle East, where they were also to create history by mounting the first-ever tank attack to take place outside Europe. (We shall look at their story later.)

Most of the crews destined for France departed from Thetford Bridge Railway Station. The site of the station now lies under and to the south of a roundabout on the A1066 road on the edge of the town, this segment of road being itself constructed on the route of the old railway track. It is, therefore, possible to identify exactly this historically important spot quite precisely.

You can stand there, as did Trevor Pidgeon, and meditate: 'From here the tank men went out to war, their singing, their banter, their cheering still audible, surely, above the noise of the present-day traffic, as their train passed down the now empty cutting leading past Culford Lodge, then on to London, to the south coast, to France, and, for some of them, to their death in the battle on the Somme'. (2)

We shall, in our imagination, go with them to France and witness their first experience of battle.

TWELVE

Arrival in France

The first group of officers and men from C Company arrived in France on 17th August and the remainder a few days later. Their tanks arrived on the 25th. D Company's officers and men arrived on the 29th and then spent two days in rest. They then moved on by train to St Riquier, from where they marched to billets in the village of Yvrench. C Company's journey must have been much the same.

One of those who encountered the shrouded tanks in France, en route to their assembly area, was Private Horace Calvert. Many years later he recorded how the inquisitiveness of himself and his comrades was successfully 'fobbed off': 'They were on the roadside covered in tarpaulin sheets; we couldn't see nothing [sic] except a square outline and there was two or three [men] around it, guarding it. And when we asked what it was, the simple reply was, 'tanks'. We naturally assumed water tanks and we'd no reason to think otherwise … Knowing the shortage of [drinking] water, we thought we were getting reserve supplies to make sure there was adequate supplies. And that was accepted by all, I believe'. (1)

Headquarters were set up in the sister village of Yvrencheux. The St Riquier tank assembly and training area as a whole, which encompassed a number of settlements, was subjected to much the same security procedures as at Elveden.

On 26th August, Field Marshall Haig travelled from his headquarters at Montreuil to watch a mock attack by about half the tanks of C Company, i.e. a dozen or so, which was carried out with 7th Battalion the Middlesex Regiment as infantry support.

Haig recorded how impressed he was by how the tanks broke through the defensive positions 'with ease' but recorded in his diary that 'we require to clear our ideas as to the tactical use of these machines'; this less than three weeks before the tanks were to undergo their baptism of fire, and despite the tank men's own ideas being, as we have seen, abundantly clear.(2) The reference to 'defensive positions' reflects the fact that a small practice area was established on ground fought over earlier, with some enhancements.

Numerous British soldiers witnessed tanks practising manoeuvring. Rifleman H.G.R. Williams of the London Rifle Brigade reflects the typical view of an infantryman in France on first encountering the new weapon: 'Before our astonished eyes appeared about six of the first Mark 1 tanks, lurching about the country on their caterpillar tracks and performing various manoeuvres, bursting through hedges, crossing trenches, demolishing walls, and even snapping off small trees.'(3)

During training in England it is highly probable that some crews had assigned nicknames to their tanks but it was here at Yvrench that the system was formalised: all C Company tanks were assigned names beginning with C and all D company with D. Numbers were assigned too. As Christy Campbell remarks in his *Band of Brigands,* C Company 'emptied the drinks cabinet': Champagne, Chartreuse, Chablis, Crème de Menthe, and Cordon Rouge. They also used names with a more personal significance, such as Clan Ruthven, or connected with historic battles, e.g. Corunna. D Company selected names such as Die Hard, Dracula, Delphine, Daphne and Dolly. Second Lieutenant Sampson, who clearly liked a pun, plumped for Delilah!

The jolly task of naming the tanks completed, and a thousand and one more onerous last-minute preparations having been made, the men from Elveden were now as ready as they could be for their initiation into war. The battle into which they were to be imminently launched, with all its historic significance for the conduct of land warfare, is known to posterity as the Battle of Flers-Courcelette. It is not intended here to give a comprehensive account of the battle, which is dealt with in detail elsewhere by numerous other writers, most especially by Trevor Pidgeon in his wonderful *The Tanks at Flers*, but to convey a general idea of what happened and to provide some 'snapshots' of, or a 'feeling' for, what the men from Elveden achieved and experienced. The next chapter, using many of their own words, will attempt to do that.

THIRTEEN

Into Battle

The British attack was planned for an eight-mile-wide section of the front a few miles to the north of Albert. Arched slightly northwards towards the Germans, the British front line was marked on the left by Thiepval and on the right by Combles. A mass of shell holes spread in every direction and few signs of civilisation remained. Woods and villages had been almost wholly destroyed by the two months of fighting which had already taken place.

The ultimate objective of the British for this new attack was to make a breakthrough in the direction of Bapaume and from there to breach the last line of the Germans' prepared defences between Morval and Le Sars, a further three to four miles to the north, and finally to exploit the gap thus created with a massive force of cavalry. Among the important features of the front to be attacked on the first day were, from west to east, Courcelette village, Martinpuich village, High Wood, Flers village, Guedecourt village, Ginchy village and a formidable German strongpoint known as the Quadrilateral – all roughly one to two miles distant from the British line.

The principal initial thrust was to be in the centre and directed, critically, at Flers. Fourth Army's commander, General Sir Henry Rawlinson, had mused on the importance of its capture ten days previously: 'In regard to Flers, I suppose the best plan is to put them [the tanks] down the main street ... and a group round either side'. (1)

In the centre and on the right the attacking force was Rawlinson's Fourth Army, which was to shoulder the main burden of the fighting, and, on the left, the Reserve Army, under General Sir Hubert Gough. In all, the available forces amounted to ten Divisions.

Forty-nine tanks were theoretically available. Six were allocated to the Reserve Army on the left to assist the Canadian Division. In the centre, twenty-six tanks were allocated to the Fourth Army, eighteen to support XV Corps, eight to support III Corps. On the right, sixteen were assigned to XIV Corps, ten of them to the Guards Division and the remaining handful split between the 6th and 56th Divisions.

However, mechanical failures, mishaps and human errors during the approach run to the start line meant that only 32 of the 49 were ultimately available to go into action. For some of the former, the approach run took nine or ten hours, the tanks grinding along in bottom gear over very difficult ground at an average speed of about half-a-mile an hour. Consequently, many crews were weary even before the first shots were fired. Drowning out even the roar of their own engines, their ears bore the noise of the huge artillery bombardment of the German lines by thousands of British artillery pieces. This had commenced three days earlier, heavy at night and intense by day, but ceasing intermittently to deprive the enemy of any sense of predictable pattern.

The 500 or so men from Elveden were part of an attacking force which, in all, numbered about 150,000 men. Spread amongst that vast force, the number of tanks ultimately in a position to go into action seems pitifully few.

Nevertheless, in Swinton's words, 'On the morning of Friday the 15th September 1916, in a ground mist which lay like a blanket over the valley of the Somme, was born a new era in land warfare. At six-twenty, zero hour, the ... tanks of C and D companies sallied forth in the attempt made by the Fourth and

Reserve Armies to revive the momentum of the Somme offensive which had already lasted for ten weeks'.

Strictly speaking, the new era had not, as Swinton says, started at 6.20 a.m. but at 5.00 a.m., for two tanks of D Company had been designated to go into action eighty minutes before their fellows to clear what was predicted to be a particularly troublesome enemy trench system known to the British as Hop Alley, near Ginchy. These pioneer tanks were D1, Daredevil, and D5, Dolphin.

Daredevil was commanded by 25-year-old Captain Harold Mortimore from Chiswick in London, whose father was an engine operator on a steamship. Mortimore had worked his way up from being an Ordinary Seaman, performing nothing more warlike than clerking duties in the Royal Navy. Most of his crew were teenagers, the youngest being Gunner Ewart Doodson from Elland in Yorkshire. Doodson was only seventeen and officially still too young even to have been recruited, let alone serve in the front line; as with many other youngsters, he must have lied successfully about his age. (Recruiting sergeants were famously ready to go along with such fabrications. A youngster clearly too young for service and not yet sufficiently guileful to lie spontaneously about his age was usually told, 'Go for a stroll around the block, lad, and come back two years older'.)

D5, Dolphin, was commanded by Lieutenant Arthur Blowers. Blowers was 25 years old, a Suffolk man (born near Saxmundham) and in civilian life a teacher. Unfortunately, Dolphin soon damaged its tail-wheel assembly on one of the shattered tree stumps which abounded and fell into a shell hole, damaging its tail-wheel steering mechanism.

D1, Daredevil, therefore had to go in alone and so, grinding slowly but successfully forward, it fell to Mortimore and his youngsters to create history alone. Mortimore later reminisced:

'There had always been a bit of rivalry at Thetford between A, B, C and D Companies as to which would be the first in action. Naturally, I was delighted when it turned out to be D, but I didn't think my tank would be the first in the company – and the first in the world – to fire a shot in anger'. (2)

Poised for action on Mortimore's segment of the line, men of the King's Own Yorkshire Light Infantry (the KOYLI) parted briefly to let Daredevil through into No Man's Land. There, in the gathering light, Mortimore could perceive the shattered remains of Delville Wood and the German trenches which were his first target. He ordered the 6-pounder gunners to open heavy fire, then turned his tank to the right to fire on the Hop Alley trench system. The men of the Yorkshire Light Infantry now rose up out of their trenches to join Daredevil in a fierce and successful attack. The surviving Germans fled and suffered terribly at the hands of Daredevil and the British infantry as they did so.

As Mortimore subsequently set down, 'We met up with the K.O.Y.L.I. all right, and set off for Delville Wood, the infantry coming along behind me along an old communications trench. I saw lots of flashes coming from the edge of the wood. I think they were machine guns but there was such an awful din going on I couldn't make out whether or not they were firing at me. I gave the order to open fire with one of the 6-pounders, but there was so much shell fire coming down in the target area that I couldn't see whether ours were doing any good or not. Anyway, I think we must have helped, because the next thing I saw was the company of K.O.Y.L.I. with fixed bayonets charging into the wood'.

One of the Yorkshire light infantrymen (Lance Corporal Len Lovell) also recorded his experiences: 'It was marvellous. That tank went on, rolling and bobbing and swaying in and out of shell holes, climbing over trees as easy as kiss-your-hand! We were awed! We were delighted that it was ours. Up to now Jerry had supplied all the surprises. Now it was his turn to be surprised!

'The tank waddled on with its guns blazing and we could see Jerry popping up and down, not knowing what to do, whether to stay or run. We bombers [i.e. men with hand grenades] were sheltering behind the tank, peering round and anxious to let Jerry have our bombs. But we had no need of them. The Jerries waited until our tank was only a few yards away and then fled – or hoped to! The tank just shot them down and the machine gun post, the gun itself, the dead and the wounded who hadn't been able to run, just disappeared. The tank went right over them. We would have danced for joy if it had been possible out there. It seemed so easy! Hop Trench was kaput and in a very few minutes Ale alley got the same treatment. We were elated'. (3)

Sergeant Major J. H. Price DCM of the King's Shropshire Light Infantry has left us his impressions, too. 'It was September 15th 1916, we had taken up our positions close to Delville Wood. During the night my C.O. came to see if the men had settled down for some rest. He then told me that in the attack the next morning we would have the help of a new weapon. I asked what form this would take and he said we would have the help of three tanks, and I asked him: "Did the general think we should be running short of water?" He replied that they were not water tanks [but ones] that held three or four men and fired machine guns and small calibre artillery weapons. Our attack was to be made on the villages of Flers and Guedecourt ... About 4.00 a.m. our guns, of all descriptions, opened up and it was like hell on earth. The Germans started replying to our bombardment and for the next two hours this continued ... It was 6.00 a.m. on the 15th September when we left our trenches and went forward, round to the east of Delville Wood, and there we saw the first tank, spitting bullets from the top of it. We had never seen anything like it before, and I think it attracted more of our attention than the enemy ... It certainly looked a monster, and it is a job for me to explain its shape, and I can only say it had huge caterpillar tracks and a large wheel [sic] behind. It went forward rather slowly and I should think it struck terror into the enemy ... [By about] mid-day ... things had quietened down somewhat. Two of our tanks were out of action, one by fire and the other, I think, by having the large wheel [sic] damaged and this I was told affected the steering. But the third tank did wonderful work, capturing Flers almost on its own...' (4)

Sergeant Major Price was right in believing the tanks must have struck terror into the enemy – the Germans were deeply shocked. One German infantryman, on the receiving end of a tank attack a little later in the war, described what it was like to encounter the novel weapons for the first time: 'One stared and stared as if one had lost the power of one's limbs. The monsters approached slowly, hobbling, rolling and rocking, but they approached. Nothing impeded them: a supernatural force seemed to propel them on. Someone in the trenches said, "The Devil is coming", and the word was passed along the line like wildfire'. (5)

Mortimore continued his advance: 'I managed to get astride one of the German trenches in front of the wood and opened fire with the Hotchkiss machine guns. There were some Germans in the dugouts and I shall never forget the looks on their faces when they emerged and saw my tank astride their trench!'

At this point, Daredevil was hit by a shell which wrecked its steering gear and thus rendered it effectively immobile, but the crew continued to bring down fire on the enemy. Later in the day, troops of the Army Service Corps were able to make their way out to the tank and assisted the crew in recovering it to the British lines.

Wrecked though they now were, Mortimore and his crew had been hugely effective in suppressing a vital German strongpoint. The Fourth Army's official report stated: 'The tank operating against the eastern corner of Delville Wood cleared up a situation that we had failed at since 15th July'.

Recalling the experience later, Mortimore said: 'Looking back on it now, I don't think I was frightened. I've been very frightened indeed, both before and after that day, but on that particular morning the whole thing seemed so unreal, besides which we all had the utmost confidence in our new weapon, the tank'.

Meanwhile, the ditched D5 had been caught up by another tank which had set off from the start line later and with its help Blowers and his men were able to extricate themselves and, albeit belatedly and handicapped by damaged steering, set off to join the action. By this time, the British had captured their First Objective, which had been virtually obliterated by extremely accurate fire by the Royal Artillery, but, despite this, serious casualties had been incurred and Blowers found the British infantry there counting their dead and tending their wounded. He and his crew did not linger but carried on to the Second Objective, which had also been taken and after a brief pause went yet further forward to support the troops attacking the Third Objective. These were men of the Rifle Brigade, the King's Royal Rifle Corps, the Oxfordshire and Buckinghamshire Light Infantry and the King's Shropshire Light Infantry. They had already suffered serious losses and the arrival of Dolphin was a morale-booster to them. (One party, Sergeant Elderfield of the King's Royal Rifle Corps and a small group of companions, had just killed the son of a German general. The son, Leutnant Kohl,

Peaceful – Flers High Street before the war.

Devastated – Flers High Street after the battle.

was the commander of two German 77 mm cannon of 7th Saxon Field Artillery Regiment, which Elderfield and his men had captured. The attack had cut down Kohl together with the bulk of his gun crews and he very quickly died of his wounds. Elderfield and his men were later to learn that to their left the Germans had earlier killed Grenadier Guards' officer Lieutenant Raymond Asquith, the eldest son of the British Prime Minister.)

Still undaunted, and firing at every likely target, Blowers and his crew ploughed on yet again until they believed they had reached Guedecourt, though it is probable they had not quite done so. At this extreme point, Blowers turned the tank around and fired at two other field guns probably also belonging to Kohl's battery. At this moment, the tank was intercepted by a risk-taking runner from the King's Shropshire Light Infantry, with a message requesting help in destroying a German strongpoint which was still holding out nearer to Flers. Blowers gave orders to the driver to change course but at this moment tragedy struck: a German shell scored a direct hit, exploding inside the tank and setting it on fire. Gutsell was killed, both of Barnsby's legs were shattered, and Foden and Thomas wounded. Barnsby died from his injuries. (The graves of the two dead men were lost but their names can be seen on the Thiepval Memorial to the Missing.) The now-impotent tank soon came under attack from some especially-resilient German infantry and it was left to Blowers to defend the survivors. He was later to tell his son Roger how he had remained in the tank firing his Webley revolver at the attackers: 'I fired over a hundred rounds. None of the targets was more than about 10 yards away, so I didn't miss many'. Blowers and the remaining survivors were eventually evacuated. He and his men had travelled farther than any other tank was to do that day. He was awarded the Military Cross for

100

'conspicuous gallantry in action' and for his and his crew's success in supporting and heartening the infantry. Corporal Foden and Private Thomas were both awarded the Military Medal for the equally gallant and successful roles they had played.

Shortly after Daredevil and Dolphin had commenced their operations, one or two other tanks with special orders had also swung into action and at the official Zero Hour of 0620 all other operational 'landships' commenced their attacks. We shall concentrate on those attacking Flers, the most essential target of the day. The principal infantry units assigned to the Flers attack were 41st and 14th Divisions, with the New Zealand Division on their left flank.

41st Division was supported by ten tanks, organised into four groups, all from D Company. The first 'group' comprised a single tank, D6 (name unknown), commanded by 2/Lt R.C. Legge, which had the doubtful privilege of leading the attack.

Behind Legge was a trio: Dolly commanded by 2/Lt. Vic Huffam; D14 (name now unknown) commanded by 2/Lt G. F. Court, who was South African; and Dinnaken (Scottish dialect, for 'Don't Understand') commanded, unsurprisingly, by a Scotsman, Lt S. H. Hastie. This group's orders were to follow Legge through Flers and then turn its attention to Guedecourt.

Behind Dolly, D14 and Dinnaken came the two final groups. One group comprised D15 (again, name unknown) commanded by Lt J. L. Bagshaw, D2 commanded by Lt H.R. Bell and D19 by Captain S.S. Sellick. The other comprised Dracula, commanded by Lt A.E. Arnold, D18 under 2/Lt L.C. Bond and D7 under Lt A. J. Enoch. This group was to attack the western side of Flers and then, similarly, assist in the capture of Guedecourt.

Four of these tanks (Sellick's, Bell's, Huffam's and

Court's) all ditched either in huge shell holes or disused dugouts. The remaining six ploughed ahead, Legge in Dolphin leading as planned. Huffam's and Court's tanks were eventually extricated, though not in time to participate in the day's action; as we shall see, their turn was to come the following morning.

Legge and his followers moved through the British front line as the dawn artillery barrage crashed down on the enemy. Infantry Sergeant Norman Carmichael of the King's Royal Rifle Corps was near to Legge's tank, and remembered '... a great flash lit up the whole of the sky behind us, and we heard a tremendous rumbling roar, followed by the sound of the coming shells, like that of an express train, culminating in a piercing shriek overhead. Then the ground in front of us seemed to heave up in a lurid burst of yellow flame, and we were on the brink of an inferno of crashing explosions. Surely there could not be a German left alive in that trench of theirs!' Unfortunately for the attacking infantry, a sufficient number did survive and inflicted grievous casualties on the attacking British. Carmichael witnessed the death of an old friend, Kidd: 'I distinctly saw poor Kidd throw up his arms, and then I knew that that loveable, generous soul, whom I had known since the very beginning [of their training], had "gone west". There were only two or three survivors in [Kidd's] section, and those very gallant fellows dragged the bodies of their killed and wounded comrades out of the path of the oncoming tank, and then went on.'

The 'oncoming tank' (Legge's) fired at every 'target of opportunity', as the army termed them. Carmichael had seen it 'lumbering past on my left, belching forth yellow flame from her Vickers gun, and making for the gap where the Flers road passed through the enemy's trench'. Carmichael was not to witness much more, being shot through the leg and tumbling into a shell hole. Almost immediately, he was to lose another comrade:

'Lance Corporal Mitchell, commander of No. 7 Section and a great favourite of mine, bent over me and inquired, "Are you alright, Sergeant?" I replied "I'm alright. Go on". No sooner were the words out of my mouth than a shrapnel shell burst ten feet over our heads. The splendid chap settled forward on his face, and there he knelt with a hole right through his head ...'

The other tanks were moving forward, too, and, like the infantry, were under heavy fire from the German guns. Bagshaw's D15 was hit and set ablaze. Two of the crew were shot and killed while escaping the flames, and others wounded. But Arnold's Dracula and Len Bond's D18 remained unscathed and continued their advance.

Meanwhile, Hastie, to the right in Dinnaken, trundled up the main road to Flers. Protecting the village were huge belts of barbed wire, in front of which and unable to penetrate it, lay the British infantry, already much reduced in numbers and continuing to suffer casualties. To the infantry's immense relief, Hastie was able to smash down the wire, move through, and literally and metaphorically crush all enemy resistance. Resistance having collapsed, the way into Flers was now open.

After destroying further German strong-points en route with its six-pounders, Dinnaken, followed by the infantry, entered the village and advanced down the gently sloping main street. This achievement was witnessed from overhead by an aircraft of the Royal Flying Corps. The aircraft returned to its base with its now-famous message of success; 'A tank is walking up the High Street of Flers with the British Army cheering behind'. Thus, Dinnaken and its crew made newspaper headlines around the world. Today, standing in the re-built and well-cared-for village that Flers now is, especially (as the author has done) on a sunny, warm and peaceful day, it is hard to imagine the carnage.

General Rawlinson's dream of the tanks taking Flers had been realised. The number of surviving infantry entering the village, though, was low, about 300. These were remnants of the King's Royal Rifle Corps, the East Surreys and the Hampshires. Later, men of the New Zealand Division came over from their positions to the west to help clear out the remaining German dugouts. (The bodies of 120 of these brave men from the other side of the world lie to this day in a cemetery nearby.)

The ever-efficient German Army was not, however, without the capacity to retaliate massively and its artillery unleashed a tremendous bombardment. Many officers and NCOs were amongst the casualties and command and control cohesion in and around the village was temporarily lost. Nevertheless, the British infantry did not abandon the place taken at such cost, and reinforcements arriving later in the day found them still established in the northern part of the village and the New Zealanders holding out in the captured German dugouts.

Hastie and his crew were lucky enough to emerge from the bombardment unscathed but their tank's engine was by now showing every sign of being about to 'pack in' under the mechanical strain of the day. Though he had reached the square at the bottom end of Flers, Hastie had little option but to order his driver to turn Dinnaken round and coax it back in the direction of the main British lines. Dinnaken was not to reach them, however, for its motor finally expired, though the driver was able to position the tank behind a sheltering bank just as it did so.

What were the Germans experiencing during all this? A surviving officer, Leutnant Braunhoffer told some of the story from his side's point of view: 'At about 8.30 a.m. the British had already overwhelmed half of Flers … A short time after, a tank [which we know to have been Dinnaken] appeared on the left front of my company position which I immediately attacked with machine gun and rifle fire and also, as it came in closer, with hand-grenades. These unfortunately caused no real damage because the tank only turned slightly to the left but otherwise just carried on. He crossed the trenches in the area of the company on my left, caused us heavy losses with his flanking machine gun fire at trenches which had to a large extent been flattened without my men being able to do anything against it ... Positioning himself close to the exit from Flers, he placed the [area] under continuous machine gun fire ...' (6)

In a later part of his account Braunhoffer recorded how he subsequently came under fire from two other tanks. These must have been two of the four tanks commanded by Arnold, Bond, Brown and Pearsall respectively, but it is not possible to be sure which two. Braunhoffer: 'Well hidden by the houses and buildings ... the enemy worked round to our rear. From here and directly to our left he now attacked [again], first of all taking the entire length of our position under continuous machine gun fire and causing more heavy losses ... I succeeded in holding out until mid-day. At that time the enemy once more made a mass attack simultaneously from the left and rear ... led by a tank which, armed with small cannons, came from the flank and fired along our whole position with devastating effect. The [infantry] attack itself was carried out with hand grenades and bayonets ... It was quite impossible to hold out any longer'.

Later, at about 2.30 in the afternoon, Arnold in Dracula was involved in heavy fighting again, having been asked by an infantry commander for help in resisting a major German counter-attack. He later wrote: 'We emerged from our [temporary] lair, crossed the sunken road and went out to the front. We were rewarded with the sight of long lines of Germans advancing in open formation, and opened fire with our port side Vickers gun at 900 yards range'.

A short while later Dracula came under direct fire from a German field gun and Arnold's knee was shattered by a German bullet whilst he was outside the tank. We cannot be certain why Arnold exited the vehicle at this point, as he was too modest to record his own part in detail, but it was probably when he stopped and climbed out to take on board a New Zealander whom he described as 'sadly wounded'. Arnold was then himself rescued under the same heavy fire by a member of his crew, Gunner J. Glaister.

At this point Dracula made her way back to the main British line, both Arnold and the Kiwi in great agony, particularly as the tank jolted and swayed over the shell-pocked ground. On his return, the first medical aid Arnold received was a tumbler-full of whiskey from his commanding officer which, remembered Arnold, reduced everything to a 'nice muzzy feeling'.

Arnold was awarded the Military Cross for conspicuous gallantry throughout the day and for rescuing the New Zealander. Gunner Glaister was awarded the Distinguished Conduct Medal for showing great courage and determination throughout. Glaister must have been a very brave man indeed, for he was to be awarded the Military Medal for another action on a future occasion, though sadly suffering very severe wounds.

In the Reserve Army's area on the left, heavy fighting had also been taking place, where six tanks of C Company were supporting the Canadian Division. The six were divided into two groups of three. The first group was commanded by Captain A.M. Inglis. His tank was Crème de Menthe (male); the others were Chartreuse (male) under 2nd/Lt.S.D.H. Clark and Chablis (female) under 2nd/Lt.G.O.L. Campbell. The second group comprised Champagne (male) under Lt.A.J.C. Wheeler, Cognac (female) under Lt. F.W. Bluemel and Cordon Rouge (female) under 2nd/Lt. J. Allen.

The Sugar Factory prior to its almost total destruction.

A prime feature of the stretch of German line allotted to these tanks was the Sugar Factory at Courcelette, which measured roughly 150 by 300 hundred metres and was very heavily fortified. It lay amidst ground pounded into something resembling a 'storm-tossed sea, a fearful place for men who had trained in the gentler fields of Elveden' as Trevor Pidgeon puts it. Champagne soon 'bellied' and the crew strived for four hours to dig it out despite intense German shellfire but in the end had to abandon the task as hopeless. At this moment, Gunner Brotherwood was struck by shrapnel and died almost immediately from loss of blood. Cognac, its steering damaged by German artillery, also bellied: the crew spent almost the entire day digging it out under heavy fire and succeeded in moving it forward a considerable distance. However, they finally had to abandon it when it fell into a trench.

However, Cordon Rouge survived the German counter-fire and as it advanced used its machine-guns to destroy a number of German machine-gun emplacements, thus greatly helping the Canadian infantry. It then went on to the Sugar Factory and again hugely assisted by destroying more machine-guns there and by cutting-off the German infantry's route of retreat. 2nd/Lt. Allen was awarded the Military Cross. (In considering the help effected by tanks in destroying machine-guns, it should be borne in mind that a single, well-sited machine-gun, operated by a determined and courageous crew, such as the Germans were almost without exception, could hold up and devastate a whole infantry battalion.)

Of the other group of three tanks, the steering mechanism of Chartreuse was damaged by shellfire and she lurched into a shell-hole. The crew worked for over three hours on digging-out, a task in which they succeeded, only to have the engine seize up on them. Chablis was also damaged by shell-fire but in any case had been experiencing irremediable mechanical problems with its tracks.

This left as the sole survivor Crème de Menthe, commanded by Captain Inglis. Despite one of its tail wheels having been blown off by a German shell, it advanced to the Sugar Factory, firing at all targets of opportunity en route. Inglis used his Hotchkiss six-pounders and the tank itself to smash through walls and destroy more enemy machine-gun nests. (Amazingly, a picture of Crème de Menthe advancing across the shell-torn mud to its Sugar Factory target was taken by a stout-hearted war photographer, Frederick Oscar Bovill. A shell can be seen bursting in the background at the moment the photo was taken, though at this point it seems to have both its tail wheels intact.)

Tank 'Crème de Menthe' moving forward to attack the Sugar Factory. Note the shell burst to the left. This photograph was probably taken, at great personal risk, by a war photographer called Frederick Oscar Bovill.

An elated Private M. M. Hood of 24th Battalion Victoria Rifles of Canada recalled: '... we saw something never before seen in warfare ... A party of us had to rush up with more bullets and grenades to the 21st Battalion, lying in shell-holes in front of the [sugar] refinery at Courcelette. As we reached them we saw a tank, what we then called a landship, named the LS Crème de Menthe, pass ahead and go right up to the walls of the refinery, its guns blazing. It seemed to lean against one of the walls which collapsed, and the monster roared into the fort, while we could see Germans streaming out behind it, offering an excellent target to the riflemen in the shell-holes.

Feldwebel [Sergeant] Weinert of the 211th Prussian Infantry Regiment, has left a record of the scene from the German point of view as the tank crews from Elveden attacked:

'A man came running in from the left, shouting "There is a crocodile crawling into our lines!" The poor wretch was off his head. He had seen a tank for the first time and had imagined the giant of a machine, rearing up and dipping down as it came, to be a monster. So the enemy had brought tanks into the lines - a new kind of fighting machine of whose existence we had no inkling and to counter which we had nothing remotely comparable. To use rifle fire against it would be like using pea-shooters'. (7)

Weinert goes on: 'Visibility was better now. On the left, level with the crossroads, was a tank; on the right, close by, was another, just in front of our weak point of junction with the 210th Regiment. It presented a fantastic picture, this Colossus, in the dawn light. One moment its front section would disappear into a crater, with the rear section still protruding, the next its yawning mouth would rear up out of the crater, to roll slowly forward with terrifying assurance. By now the pair could only have been 100 metres from our line, as dawn was giving way to daylight. All of a sudden a hail of shellfire was loosed upon us as the massed enemy batteries were directed at our thinning lines of infantry. This also seemed to be a sign for the planes and tanks, as the former strafed us from above and the latter attacked us with machine-gun fire. Using their revolving guns, the tanks sought to clear the ground in front of them. The noise was like a concert out of hell. Dead, wounded, severed arms and legs, white and naked as if straight from the hands of a sculptor, were flung far back into the lines. The trench was in turmoil and nobody could help the poor souls who were buried'.

Inglis was awarded the Distinguished Service Order. At 32 he was considerably older than the overwhelming majority of tank men. He had been born in Inverness but educated much further south at Cheltenham College. However, the achievements of Crème de Menthe would have been quite impossible without the skill and determination of its driver, Acting Corporal George Shepherd of the Army Service Corps. His task had been made exceptionally difficult by the damaged tail wheel yet he succeeded in manoeuvring the tank through, round or over every obstacle. For his outstanding courage and expertise he was awarded the Distinguished Conduct Medal. As to the other tank (for reports record the existence of two in this part of the action) its identity remains uncertain, lost in the mists of time. Presumably it was a tank from elsewhere on the front which had strayed from its route but which nevertheless played a brave and important role.

While these momentous events had been taking place, the stranded Huffam and Court and their crewmen climbed onto the roofs of their ditched tanks 'and watched our other tanks go in. It was a wonderful experience, a barrage of terrific intensity, the rising ground in front seemed to disappear. Jerry, dumbfounded at our firepower, only to see for the first time our tanks rolling towards him, rose from his trenches back to Flers, but even there he couldn't stop our tanks and the uplifted infantry had him out'. Huffam was conscious that taking this ground had 'previously cost tens of thousands of lives'.

In the afternoon, men from a labour battalion dug-out Huffam and Court's tanks and the two officers then reported back to their Company commander, Major Summers. He told them to prepare themselves for an attack on Guedecourt the following day, September 16th, in concert with the only other four tanks which remained operational (D2, D4, D7 and D19). The attack would take them through already-captured Flers.

'It was a lovely morning' when D14 and D9 started up early that day (the 16th), Huffam recollected. 'Then I met Court who confirmed what I'd been told, [that] the attack was cancelled. [But] we had little time to be glad,' Huffam continued, for Major

Summers soon informed them that 'those orders applied [only] to the infantry and not to tanks'. Summers additional encouraging news was that all four of the other tanks had again ditched. 'Summers was not a religious man,' recalled Huffam, 'but he ended his message with the words "God bless you." '

'Now it was two tanks, no infantry, no supporting barrage, and less than a mile away Guedecourt, known to be a strong position.' (Huffam does not end this latter sentence with an exclamation mark, but one seems justified.) The two friends then tossed a coin to determine who would take the lead. Court won and made the honourable but unenviable choice of leading on the left side of the road, Huffam following a little to the rear on the right.

'Flers was an absolute shambles', Huffam recalled in the 1960s. 'We drove down the High Street, but it was just a mass of bodies and brickwork. I made one or two attempts to get out of the tank to clear a way through the corpses, but the enemy was putting down some pretty heavy artillery fire and I had to give up. My driver was a lad called Archer and he was pretty sickened when I gave the order to advance over these bodies, but there wasn't much else we could do except plough straight over the lot.

Just in the middle of the High Street an officer came running out to meet us, waving his arms madly, so I stopped and opened one of the ports to hear what he was trying to say to us. But all he said was: "For God's sake, take your bloody stinkbox out of here, it's drawing fire on us." '

Peering through his glass prism, Huffam suddenly saw 'a damned great crater in the way. There was a way round, but it was blocked by a big Bavarian grinning hugely and holding his arms up in surrender. I couldn't drive round him or I would have bellied in the crater; I couldn't just drive over him alive, so I ordered Archer to shoot him. Archer shouted "I can't", so the only thing left was for me to shoot him myself, which I did, and then we were able to get on'. (It is pertinent to point out that killing a surrendering man, then or now, is against the laws of war, but how frequently have such laws been flouted in the heat of battle, and not infrequently afterwards.)

Flers High Street today. It would have been about here that Vic Huffam took the decision to shoot a German soldier.

Shortly after leaving the north of the village, the two tanks encountered very heavy artillery fire: Court's tank was 'smothered in shells' and Huffam's driver, the gentle, humane Archer, suddenly threw up his hands to his blood-covered face and yelled, 'I can't see'.

He had been blinded by shell splinters. 'I managed to get him out of the seat,' said Huffam, 'and got Corporal Sanders, my

NCO gearsman, to take his place. He wanted to know which way to go but all I could do was to tell him to follow Court.' He was not to follow Court for long: a minute or two later Court's tank received a direct hit and 'immediately exploded'. All eight members of the crew were killed or mortally wounded.

In spite of the shock of witnessing D14's fate, Huffam's Dolly continued firing. She was by now almost astride the enemy's 'Flea' trench, with the 'two starboard guns doing terrible execution of the bewildered Germans'. But she was then struck by German fire and the port guns fell silent. Huffam tried to attract the gunners' attention by leaning over and kicking them, but they were never to fire again, both being dead. Thus perished 19-year-old Private Ron Chapple and 28-year-old Private Alf Andrew.

Huffam recorded, 'We were all in bad shape', every remaining man being wounded or shell-shocked. Dolly was then struck again, this time by a larger shell. 'There was an explosion, then fire, and I came round to find myself lying [in the mud, outside the tank] on top of my corporal,' whose shinbones were sticking out from the flesh. 'For Christ's sake get off my legs, sir', cried the corporal, Harold Sanders. 'I had been issued with morphine tablets and I quietened him with these and bandaged him with first aid dressings from the others of my crew'. Huffam himself had been blown through the top of the tank and lost his teeth, hair and eyebrows.

'Sanders was in a bad way. I'd given him perhaps too much morphia to quieten his cries, but I knew I had to get him back and, to help him and myself, I fastened my belt to his, and as I crawled from hole to hole he came with me.' As they neared the British front line, their struggles were spotted and they were brought in under shellfire by some Guardsmen and Durham Light Infantrymen.

Both of Sanders legs had to be amputated but he survived and six months later was visited by Huffam in a Kentish hospital, Huffam finding Sanders in the entrance hall in a wheelchair, to which he was to be confined for the rest of his days. While in hospital himself, in Oxford, Huffam received a visit from Mrs Court, Court's mother, who still held out some hope of her son being alive despite him and his crew having all been posted as 'missing believed killed'. It fell to Huffam to tell Mrs Court that her son was truly dead. As to the dead men of Huffam's crew, they, like Court and his men and so many others, have no known graves but their names can be found on the massive Memorial to the Missing at Thiepval.

One other significant event of the day must be recorded, a 'friendly fire' incident which will resonate with present-day readers accustomed to news of such tragedies in Afghanistan and Iraq. Bert Chaney, who was a signaller with the 7th London Territorial battalion recorded what occurred on his section of the front: 'Instead of going to the German lines, the three tanks assigned to us straddled our front line, stopped and then opened up with a murderous machine gun fire, enfilading us left and right. There they sat, squat monstrous things, noses stuck up in the air, crushing the sides of our trench out of shape with their machine guns swiveling around and firing like mad. Everyone dived for cover, except the colonel. He jumped on top of the parapet, shouting at the top of his voice: "Runner, runner, go and tell those tanks to stop firing at once. At once, I say". By now the [Germans'] fire had risen to a crescendo but, giving no thought to his personal safety as he saw the tanks firing at his own men, he ran forward and furiously rained blows with his cane on the side of one of the tanks in an endeavor to attract their attention. Although, what with the sounds of the engines and firing in such an enclosed space, no one in the tank could hear him, they finally realised they were on the wrong trench and moved on, scaring the Jerries out of their wits and making them scuttle like rabbits.'

History does not record the number of losses suffered in the incident; as Chaney makes no mention of casualties, it is to be hoped they were minimal, though the use of the word 'murderous' may imply otherwise. (9)

In conclusion, it must be said that we have followed only a handful of the stories of the men from Elveden who went into action on those two historic days of 15th and 16th September 1916, but it is hoped that a representative account has been rendered of what those pioneering crews did and saw and felt as they endured their baptism.

The price of war. The burnt and mangled body of a British tankman.

Now let us now stand back from the personal experiences

and briefly review events 'in the round'.

First, the raw figures. Of the 32 tanks which had reached the start line on the 15th:

nine advanced in front of or with the infantry

nine followed the infantry

nine broke down

five became 'ditched'.

Second, let us look at the effect of the tanks on the British infantrymen. As we have seen, they were hugely impressed and heartened by the new monsters. One soldier of the Liverpool Scottish Regiment summed up the general view: 'Of course, I was only a lad at the time but to see those damned great things snorting and rolling their way through the mud, machine-guns sticking out everywhere and all firing at once - no wonder Jerry ran! I'd have run if they'd been on the other side'.

Third, let us consider the effect on the enemy. The views of the German soldiers, generally men of superb and resourceful fighting qualities, have been illustrated by extracts from their own testimonies and it is fair to say they became haunted by the thought of further attacks. The Chief of Staff of the 3rd German Army Group promptly endorsed the view of the man in the trench: 'The enemy in the latest fighting have employed new engines of war as cruel as they are effective'.

Fourth, in an abundance of instances the tanks had demonstrated their effectiveness and achieved tactical success despite the complete absence of battle experience of their crews. They had been instrumental in minimising infantry casualties, grievous though these were. In particular, and despite all the difficulties of the day, the tanks had achieved what General Rawlinson had dreamed of – putting a tank down the main street of the prime target, Flers.

In summary, these achievements, though tentative and by

no means overwhelming, were highly encouraging for the future. But why was it that the tanks on 15th September were not able to succeed in their overall objectives? There are two main reasons.

First, there was the immaturity of the tank as a mechanical device. By definition, the stresses and strains of battle on mechanical designs and components cannot be properly tested until battle itself has taken place, and many tanks simply broke down. However, it should be noted that great improvements in reliability and general technical effectiveness were soon to be achieved in the light of experience.

Second, the number of tanks available was very limited and even this number was unwisely split up into even smaller packets. As we have seen, the deep feeling of the leaders of the new tank arm had been that the weapon should not have been introduced to the battlefield until it was available in much larger numbers than at Flers, and even then used only in a concentrated, as opposed to a dispersed, way. This view, of course, did not prevail.

In sum, the first use of this small number of tanks had proved beyond doubt their potential, and the courage and efficiency of their crews, but had not been decisive. Had patience been exercised by the ultimate decision-takers, hundreds of tanks could have been unleashed in a surprise and mass attack a few months later, with possibly devastating results. As it was, the element of surprise had been lost. But against that, it can be argued that unleashing a massive force without first experimenting with a small one could have led to a widespread calamity – especially in regard to mechanical failure. (Reliability was rapidly improved in the light of the lessons learned at Flers-Courcellette.) It is easy to make decisions with hindsight; prolonged, conscientious and intelligent thought at the time can still get things wrong, a problem that military commanders have struggled with throughout the ages.

This account has confined itself to only the first two days of the Battle of Flers-Courcelette because of their war-changing significance. But the Battle as a whole, a phase of the Somme offensive, was to go on for another fortnight and, despite some overall gains, was to end ultimately in inconclusive results. The Battle of the Somme in its entirety did not end until November.

FOURTEEN

From Elveden to Palestine:
the first tank action outside Europe

We shall now learn a little more of what might be called the 'Palestine Party'. Whilst war was raging in mainland Europe in 1916, the British were also engaged in a major struggle with the Turkish (Ottoman) Empire in the Middle East. When the war had broken out, the Turks, historically suspicious of Russian expansionism, reached the conclusion that as the Russians had placed themselves in the British and French camp, it would be wise for them as Turks to do the opposite. The Germans thus gained a powerful ally, the Turks being a people who had ruled huge tracts of the Middle East (including Palestine) for four or more centuries and with a reputation as formidable soldiers. As is well known, in early 1915 they were bloodily to repulse Britain and her Dominion partners at Gallipoli.

In the autumn of 1916, at about the time C and D Companies were leaving Elveden for France, it was decided to bolster the British advance on Turkish-held Syria by sending a detachment of twelve tanks to reinforce the infantry, cavalry and armoured car units operating there. E Company was selected to supply most of the men and Major Nutt, who had previously served with an armoured car detachment in Egypt, was appointed as commander. The detachment comprised 22 officers and 226 other ranks and had its own comprehensive maintenance and repair section, for it was obvious that, so far from home support, the unit would have to rely very much on its own resources and ingenuity. Thus it was equipped with two Holt tractors, sponson trolleys, workshop trailers, two lorries and a copious supply of spare parts. The Palestine party left Elveden in December, the personnel making the traditional departure from Thetford Bridge Station and going on board ship at Devonport. The tanks and workshop were sent to Avonmouth for despatch to Egypt, from whence they were to travel on to Palestine.

Because of the far-flung nature of the expedition, care had been taken to equip the unit with tanks in first-rate order. Thus were selected a dozen tanks delivered from the manufacturers only recently and little used in training. All were fully serviced and with any minor faults fully rectified. Whilst this was being done, eight other tanks, 'tired', worn and requiring repairs and maintenance, were being readied for transport from Elveden down to Hampshire where a new and even larger training ground was being prepared, it already being evident that the tank arm would grow immensely.

There now occurred one of those monumental 'cock-ups' which the British Army likes to reminisce about (sometimes with greater relish than for any of its successes). Somehow, the twelve first-rate tanks destined for the Middle East were sent to Hampshire and the eight old, worn and un-serviced ones loaded onto the freighter at Avonmouth and sent to Egypt. Who was to blame, military or civilians, the Army or the railway companies, is now lost in the mists of time.

On arrival at Avonmouth the old tanks were still covered in mud, hundredweights of it adhering to each. By further mis-fortune, the tanks were placed in the ship's hold next to the intense heat generated by the engine room. Thus the mud was baked at high temperature for a month and by the time of unloading in Egypt had become as hard as rock. It had to be chipped-off with hammers and chisels, the mud on and around the tracks being especially pestilential. Some of the vehicles could not be moved for more than a week. (Thus the DNA of ancient Elveden mud must still linger somewhere in the dust of Egypt even today.)

The mud at last removed, workshop men and crews alike set about intensively 're-fettling' the tanks as best they could with the means at their disposal, and urgent signals were sent back to the UK calling for despatch of more spare parts. The ingenuity and determination of the workshop teams was agreed to be beyond praise.

There was to be perhaps only one consolation for these harassed crews and mechanics: the reviled daily job of greasing the tank tracks was found in the new conditions to be quite unnecessary, indeed counter-productive. On French battlefields, mud, grit and stones lodged everywhere, causing destructive friction in the tracks and sprockets, but in the desert the dry sand simply ran out of the tracks like water.

That was possibly the only benefit the crews obtained from operating in the Middle East, for the heat made the already appalling conditions inside the tanks well-nigh unendurable. 'On account of the heat no movement of tanks, save in battle or some other exceptional circumstance, took place after eight o'clock in the morning,' wrote Captain D.G. Browne M.C. in his memoirs.(1) Tanks were also driven without their sponsons whenever possible in order to provide some illusion of ventilation, though the desert air going in was often of a similar temperature to the engine-heat coming out. Moreover, the tanks in motion created choking clouds of dust. A ditty summing-up the Army's view of Palestine in general was:

Dust in heaps and dust in piles, dust in shifting ridges;
Dust and dust for miles and miles, and what ain't dust is
    midges.(2)

By March 1917, the British had advanced near to the city of Gaza but failed to take it at the first attempt. Shortly thereafter, the Elveden men arrived at the front and it was in the Second Battle of Gaza, 17th to 19th April, that they first used the (doubtful) power of their worn tanks to assist the infantry. Compounding the difficulties was the fact that the very few tanks available were simply given too much to do, each one, for example, having to cover about forty miles of desert.

These men must have felt an incredibly long way from Elveden, especially as most of them would not have been overseas previously in those days of rare foreign travel.

Four tanks were detailed for the first phase of the battle, four of them to assist the 52nd Division if needed (they were not) and two to lead the troops of 54th Division. Captain Browne again: 'The tanks [lacking a covered approach] came under observation soon after dawn, before they had reached the enemy's trenches and one soon received a direct hit. Two of the crew were killed and an officer lost an eye from a splinter. The hostile guns now concentrated on [this] derelict machine which, after it had been abandoned, was hit again and again, set on fire and destroyed. The second tank however, was able to carry out its task of clearing the trenches to the north and north-west of the ridge [on which the enemy had been dug in], giving the infantry valuable help. When the position was consolidated the tank returned [to its start line]. The members of the crew, who had been in the tank for fourteen hours, were completely exhausted. In such conditions of heat as they suffered, their gallantry and endurance were remarkable'.

Note the greatcoat hug on the side of the tank. Fiercely hot in the daytime, the deserts were bone-chillingly cold at night.

The handful of surviving tanks returned to the attack forty-eight hours later in the second phase of the battle, embarking against Turkish positions on the ten-mile long ridge of Ali Muntar, a spine of sandy hills covered with cactus scrub. Inevitably, some of this handful of mechanically-weary landships broke down. One tank, Tiger, however, penetrated far forward, having fired 27,000 rounds of ammunition. The second-in-command of the Palestine Detachment, Major O.A. Forsyth-Major wrote of Tiger in his report: 'All the crew, including the officer, were wounded and all, except the [wounded] officer, who took the driver's place, were in a state of complete collapse as a result of six hours' continuous strain under heavy fire'. (3)

There were other stories which could be told of the Gaza action, but suffice to say that the crews (which incurred a forty per cent casualty rate) were recognised as setting the highest standards in attempting to help the infantry under these most trying conditions. One particular example of bravery stands out: a tank was set on fire by a direct hit but three men from another tank rushed across and pulled the tank's commander and four of the crew out of the flames. They then succeeded in carrying the five men back under heavy fire to comparative safety in a trench about two hundred metres to the rear. They then returned to the tank over the bullet-swept ground to remove the machine-guns from the blazing machine. All three men, Lance-Corporal V. Hatherall and Privates P. Janes and J. Oldknow, were awarded the Distinguished Conduct Medal.

Despite all of the men having done their best in the face of every kind of difficulty, post-battle assessments of the tanks were agreed in judging them to have been of limited effectiveness. This is hardly surprising given their condition and the paucity of their numbers.

It should be noted that the British did go on to take Gaza in a third battle and that the growing numbers of new and improved tanks they unleashed in what is now modern-day Israel, Jordan, Iraq, and Syria, greatly assisted the British Army in entirely evicting the long-dominant Turks from these strategic territories. In short, tanks were soon to prove highly effective in the prevailing desert conditions of the Middle East. So much so, in fact, that today, and not to its benefit, the whole region is awash with them.

The author's elder son at the Tank Corps memorial, Flers-Courcelette

FIFTEEN

From Flers to Final Victory

Historic though it was, we have seen that on the face of it the baptism of fire of the men from Elveden achieved no more than a limited tactical success. We have also seen that the causes were diverse: the small number of tanks employed; their mechanical unreliability at this initial stage of development; and, crucially, the decision not to hold back until they could be deployed in formidable numbers in a surprise attack over suitable terrain.

Even so, the Flers operations did prove to those with open minds that the potential of the new weapon was vast. Unfortunately, open minds were still not a universal phenomenon and not a few senior officers persisted in their misguided view that tanks were either toys or that, strategically and tactically, they could be deployed in ways superior to those recommended by the tank specialists.

Consequently, though tanks were used in increasing numbers during the remainder of 1916 and most of 1917, results were mixed. At Arras, a decent, though not great, success was achieved. But on the battlefields of Ypres and Passchendale in the massive offensives of 1917, the reputation of the tank suffered a major and unfair setback. Here the flouting of the tank men's thinking was perverse to the extent that the 30-ton vehicles were ordered to operate in pools of liquid mud, flooded fields and water-filled shell craters. In these conditions, it was not only tanks but infantrymen and horses that floundered (and not infrequently drowned).

Against this unpromising background, General Elles (who had by now taken over command of the tank arm from Swinton) and his comrades nevertheless succeeded in building up a large tank fleet. By dint of persistence they gradually increased, too, their influence on the decision-making processes. They were eventually successful to the degree that on 20th November 1917 the first-ever truly massed tank attack was made at Cambrai. For this long-desired venture, almost 500 machines were gathered together in astonishing stealth to avoid giving the enemy any inkling of an impending attack. For the same reason a preliminary artillery bombardment was entirely foregone. And, at last, the ground chosen was good 'tank country'.

The British attack was devastating. The German lines collapsed and the tanks and their supporting infantry made an advance to a depth and at a speed unprecedented since the onset of the largely-static battle lines of late 1914. The victory was so complete that church bells, silenced since the outbreak of war, were rung throughout Britain in celebration. However, there was a 'but': almost as if the British were surprised by the scale of their own success, forces adequate to hold the conquered ground were brought up neither at sufficient speed nor in sufficient quantities to prevent the Germans re-capturing it before many days were out. Thus the tanks' gains were sadly wasted.

Nevertheless, Cambrai was an historic success: there was now no-one in the British Army (or any other army, at any level) who was not completely convinced of the power of tanks when properly employed in suitable conditions.

Following the ultimate failure of the titanic German attacks of March and April 1918 – their final attempt to break the Allied lines – the British and French returned to the offensive. From this time on, fluid warfare was restored, and in the final months of the war the tanks came into their own as weapons of armoured and mobile firepower and instruments of mass intimidation.

Amongst so much that could be said, special mention should perhaps be made of the pivotal role of the tanks on 8th

August 1918. This day was described by General Ludendorff, the German Commander-in-Chief, as 'the Black Day of the German Army in the history of the war'. On this day, he and his senior staff privately acknowledged that the war would be lost.

Shortly thereafter, General Wrisberg, speaking in the Reichstag on behalf of the Minister of War (General Scheuch), said: 'The attack on August 8 ... was not unexpected by our leaders. When, nevertheless, the English succeeded in achieving a great success the reasons are to be sought in the massed employment of Tanks and surprise under the protection of fog.'

The Germans were very late in developing tanks in response to the British innovation, and manufactured not many more than 100. Here German troops hitch a ride.

On the British side, and way down the scale of rank, Captain Douglas Browne summarised the day in this way: 'When, at 4.20 am ... there appeared suddenly out of this veil [of smoke and mist] over 330 heavy tanks [supported by nearly 100 light ones and a fleet of armoured cars], followed closely by lines of skirmishers and then by the main waves of the assault, the German front for twelve miles was rent like a cobweb'.

As a consequence of this devastating success, and always supported by the tanks, the British and Dominion troops and their allies were enabled to embark on the triumphant series of advances that marked the last 100 days of war.

By mid-October the German High Command had no alternative but to officially report to the Reichstag, (the German Parliament), in the following terms:

The Higher Command has been compelled to come to the enormously difficult decision that in all human probability there is no longer any prospect of forcing the enemy to sue for peace.

Two factors have had a decisive influence on our decision, namely, tanks and our reserves.

The enemy has made use of tanks in unexpectedly large numbers. In cases where they have suddenly emerged from smoke-clouds our men were completely unnerved ... Solely owing to the success of the tanks we have suffered enormous losses ...

A few days' later, the nascent German Wireless Service published a statement by General Scheuch personally: 'The superiority of the enemy is principally due to their use of tanks.'

Haig agreed, stating: '... the importance of the part played by [the tanks] in breaking the resistance of the German infantry can scarcely be exaggerated.'

Three weeks later, on 11th November 1918, the Armistice was signed and the Germans and their allies laid down their arms. The men of Elveden had finally triumphed. It may be said, in the words of the unofficial motto of the Tank Corps, that they had come 'from mud, through blood, to the green fields beyond'.

A poster advertising a musical 'The Byng Boys' (General Byng).
Compare this jolly portrayal of tank warfare with Siegfried Sassoon's
poem, 'Blighters' in the Epilogue.

APPENDIX

The First Tank Against Tank Action

We have accompanied, in our minds, the first tankmen to go to France and the first to serve outside Europe. Both events were historic but, for completeness in the matter of 'firsts', one other event should be recorded: the first battle of tank against tank, even though this was not directly connected with Elveden. The graphic account here given is taken from the account by tank commander Captain (then 2nd Lieutenant) Frank Mitchell M.C. about his experiences in the Great War. (It should be noted that whilst Mitchell did not train at Elveden, it is possible that one or more members of his crew had done so but this has not so far been confirmed.)

The German tanks Mitchell and his comrades engaged were of the A7V type, the only model the Germans used operationally in the course of the war, apart from a number captured from the British which were repaired and re-painted in German colours. Of their own A7Vs, only 100 were ordered and a mere twenty delivered. Even these twenty reached the battlefields late – which is all rather surprising in view of the Germans' mastery of tank warfare later on.

The A7V was a cumbersome machine, weighing 36 tons, 7.34 metres (24.1 feet) long and 3.3 metres (11 feet) high. Maximum speed from its two Daimler Benz 4-cylinder engines was 4 mph across country and 9 mph on roads. It had a curiously large crew of 18 men: the commander (usually an officer), driver, mechanic, mechanic/signaller, six machine-gunners and six loaders and two artillerymen as gunner and loader for its 57mm cannon.

Mitchell's encounter with the A7Vs was on the 24th April 1918, a month or so after the Germans had unleashed Operation Michael, the stupendous attack which they hoped would turn the tide in their favour and lead to final victory. To secure this, German forces on the Western Front had been massively reinforced by regiments brought back from the East following the collapse of Russia. The German intention was to drive a huge wedge between the British and French armies, thus placing the Allies in an irrecoverable situation.

Mitchell's encounter took place between Cachy and Villers-Bretenneux, near Amiens, and he and his men had already been badly affected by a barrage of German gas shells; consequently the crew had already been reduced to five. The situation at the British front line was desperate, and Mitchell's account of his part in events gives not only a vivid picture of the first tank against tank action but of the bravery and barbarity of tank warfare generally. Mitchell's principal opponent was 39-year-old Second Lieutenant Wilhelm Blitz, in civilian life a Professor of Chemistry. According to Mitchell's account:

'The order came: "Proceed to the Cachy switch-line and hold it at all costs." We put on our gas masks once more and plunged, like divers, into the gas-laden wood. As we struggled to crank up, one of the ... men collapsed. We put him against a tree, and gave him some tablets of ammonia to sniff, and then, as he did not seem to be coming round, we left him for time was pressing. Out of a crew of seven there remained only four men, with red-rimmed bulging eyes, while my second reserve driver, had had only a fortnight's driving experience. Fortunately one gearsman was [then] loaned to me from another tank.

'The three tanks [forming the attack group], one male armed with two 6-pounder guns and two females, armed with machine guns only, crawled out of the wood and set off over the open ground towards Cachy, Captain Brown coming in my tank.

'Ahead loomed the German barrage, a menacing wall of fire in our path. There was no break in it anywhere. Should I go straight ahead and trust to luck? It seemed impossible that we could pass through that deadly area unhit. I decided to attempt a zigzag course, as somehow it seemed safer.

'Luck was with us. At top speed we went safely through the danger zone and soon reached the Cachy lines; but there was no sign of our infantry. Suddenly, out of the ground ten yards away, an infantryman arose, waving his rifle furiously. We stopped. He ran forward and shouted through the flap 'Look out, Jerry tanks about!' Swiftly he disappeared into the trench again and Captain Brown immediately got out and ran across the heavily shelled ground to warn the female tanks.

'I informed the crew, and a great thrill ran through us all. Opening a loophole, I looked out. There, some three hundred yards away, a round, squat-looking monster was advancing; behind it came waves of infantry and farther away to the left and right crawled two more of these armed tortoises.

'So we had met our rivals at last! For the first time in history tank was encountering tank! The 6-pounder gunners crouching on the floor, their backs against the engine cover, loaded their guns expectantly.

'We still kept a zigzag course, threading the gaps between the lines of hastily-dug trenches, and coming near the small protecting belt of barbed wire, we turned left, and the right gunner, peering through his narrow slit, made a sighting shot. The shell burst some distance beyond the leading enemy tank. No reply came. A second shot boomed out, landing just to the right but again there was no reply. More shots followed.

'Suddenly a hurricane of hail pattered against our steel wall, filling the interior with myriads of sparks and flying splinters.

Something rattled against the steel helmet of the driver sitting next to me, and my face was stung with minute fragments of steel. The crew flung themselves flat on the floor. The driver ducked his head and drove straight on.

'Above the roar of our engine sounded the staccato rat-tat-tat-tat of machine guns, and another furious jet of bullets sprayed our steel side, the splinters clanging against the engine cover. The Jerry tank had treated us to a broadside of armour-piercing bullets!

'Taking advantage of a dip in the ground, we got beyond range, and then turning, we manoeuvred to get the left gunner on the moving target. Owing to our gas casualties the gunner was working single-handed, and his right eye being swollen with gas, he aimed with the left. Moreover, as the ground was heavily scarred with shell holes, we kept going up and down like a ship in a heavy sea, which made accurate shooting difficult. His first shot fell some fifteen yards in front, the next went beyond, and then I saw the shells bursting all around the enemy tank. He fired shot after shot in rapid succession every time it came into view.

'Nearing the village of Cachy, I noticed to my astonishment that the two females were slowly limping away to the rear. Almost immediately on their arrival they had both been hit by shells which had torn great holes in their sides, leaving them defenceless against machine gun bullets, and as their Lewis guns were useless against the armour-plate of the enemy they could do nothing but withdraw.

'Now the battle was to us, with our infantry in their trenches tensely watching the duel, like spectators in the pit of a theatre. For a moment they became uncomfortably more than spectators. As we turned and twisted to dodge the enemy's shells I looked down to find that we were going into a trench full of British soldiers, who were huddled together and yelling at the tops of their voices to attract our attention. A quick signal to the gearsman seated in the rear of the tank and we turned swiftly, avoiding catastrophe by a second.

'Then came our first casualty. Another raking broadside from the German tank, and the rear Lewis gunner was wounded in both legs by an armour-piercing bullet which tore through our steel plate. We had no time to put on more than a temporary dressing, and he lay on the floor, bleeding and groaning, whilst the 6-pounder boomed over his head and the empty shell cases clattered all round him.

'The roar of our engine, the nerve-wracking rat-tat-tat of our machine guns blazing at the Boche infantry, and the thunderous boom of our 6-pounders, all bottled up in that narrow space, filled our ears with tumult, while the fumes of petrol and cordite half stifled us. We turned again and proceeded at a slower pace. The left gunner, registering carefully, began to hit the ground right in front of the German tank. I took a risk and stopped the tank for a moment. The pause was justified; a well-aimed shot hit the enemy's conning tower, bringing him to a standstill. Another roar and yet another white puff at the front of the tank denoted a second hit! Peering with his swollen eyes through the narrow slit, the gunner shouted words of triumph that were drowned by the roar of the engine. Then he aimed with great deliberation and hit for the third time. Through a loophole I saw the tank heel over to one side; then a door opened and out ran the crew. We had knocked the monster out!

'Quickly I signed to the machine gunner, and he poured volley after volley into the retreating figures. My nearest enemy being out of action, I turned to look at the other two, who were coming forward slowly, while our 6-pounder guns spread havoc in the ranks of the advancing German infantry with round after round of case-shot, which scattered like the charge of a shotgun.

'Now, I thought, we shall not last very long. The two great tanks were creeping relentlessly forward; if they both concentrated their fire on us at once we would be finished. We fired rapidly at the nearest tank, and to my intense joy and amazement I saw it slowly back away. Its companion also did not appear to relish a fight, for it turned and followed its mate, and in a few minutes they had both disappeared, leaving our tank the sole possessor of the field.

'The situation, however gratifying, soon displayed numerous disadvantages. We were now the only thing above ground, and naturally the German artillery made savage efforts to wipe us off the map. Up and down we went, followed by a train of bursting shells. I was afraid that at any minute a shell would penetrate the roof and set the petrol alight, making the tank a roaring furnace before we could escape.

'Then I saw an aeroplane flying overhead not more than a hundred feet up. A great black cross was on each underwing and, as it crossed over us, I could see clearly the figures of the pilot and the observer. Something round and black dropped from it. For a fraction of a second I watched it, horrified: the front of the tank suddenly bounded up into the air, and the whole machine seemed to stand on end. Everything shook, rattled, jarred with an earth quaking shock. We fell back with a mighty crash, and then continued on our journey unhurt. Our steel walls had held nobly, but how much more would they endure?

'A few minutes later, as we were turning, the driver failed to notice that we were on the edge of a steep shell hole, and down we went with a crash, so suddenly that one of the gunners was thrown forward on top of me. In order to right the tank, the driver jerked open the throttle to its fullest extent. We snorted up the opposite lip of the crater at full speed, but when just about to clamber over the edge the engine stopped. Our nose was pointing heavenwards, a lovely stationary target for the Boche artillery.

'A deadly silence ensued …

'After the intolerable racket of the last few hours it seemed to us uncanny. Now we could hear the whining of shells, and the vicious crump as they exploded near at hand. Fear entered our hearts; we were inclined at such a steep angle that we found it impossible to crank up the engine again. Every second we expected to get a shell through the top. Almost lying on their sides, the crew strained and heaved at the starting handle, but to no effect.

'Our nerves were on edge; there was but one thing left, to put the tank in reverse gear, release the rear brake, and run backwards down the shell hole under our own weight. Back we slid, and happily the engine began to splutter, then, carefully nursing the throttle, the driver changed gear and we climbed out unhurt. What sweet music was the roar of the engine in our ears now!

'But the day was not yet over. As I peeped through my flap I noticed that the German infantry were forming up some distance away, preparing for an attack. Then my heart bounded with joy, for away on the right I saw seven small Whippets, the newest and fastest type of tank, unleashed at last and racing into action. They came on at six to eight miles an hour, heading straight for the Germans, who scattered in all directions, fleeing terror-stricken from this whirlwind of death. The Whippets plunged into the midst of them, ran over them, spitting fire into their retreating ranks.

'Their work was soon over. Twenty-one men in seven small tanks overran some twelve hundred of the enemy and killed at least four hundred, nipping an attack in the bud. Three of the seven came back, their tracks dripping with blood; the other four were left burning out there in front, and their crews could not hope to be made prisoners after such slaughter. One broke down not far from Cachy, and I saw a man in overalls get out, and, with a machine gun under his arm, run to another Whippet, which stopped to pick him up.

'We continued to cruise to and fro in front of the Cachy switch-line, and presently a fourth German tank appeared, about eight hundred yards away. The left gunner opened fire immediately, and a few minutes later the reply came swift and sharp, three shells hitting the ground alongside of us. Pursuing the same tactics as before, we increased our speed and then turned, but the Jerry tank had disappeared; there was to be no second duel.

'Later on, when turning again, we heard a tremendous crack, and the tank continued to go round in a circle. "What the blazes are you doing?" I roared at the driver in exasperation. He looked at me in bewilderment and made another effort, but still we turned round and round. Peeping out, I saw one caterpillar track doubled high in the air. We had been hit by the Boche artillery at last, two of the track plates being blown clean away!

'I decided to quit. The engine stopped. Defiantly we blazed away our last few rounds at the slopes near Villers-Bretonneux and then crept gingerly out of the tank, the wounded man riding on the back of a comrade.

'We were making for the nearest trench when - rat-tat-tat-tat - the air became alive with bullets. We flopped to the ground, waiting breathlessly whilst the bullets threw up the dirt a few feet away. When the shooting ceased we got up again and ran forward. By a miracle nothing touched us, and we reached the parapet of a trench. Our faces were black with grime and smoke, and our eyes bloodshot. The astonished infantrymen gazed at us open-mouthed, as if we were apparitions from a ghostly land. "Get your bayonets out of the way," we yelled, and tumbled down into the trench.'

Mitchell was awarded the Military Cross and his sergeant, 'a courageous and cool-headed Scot named McKenzie,' was awarded the Military Medal.

EPILOGUE

1. British

'Blighters'
by Siegfried Sassoon

The House is crammed: tier beyond tier they grin
And cackle at the Show, while prancing ranks
Of harlots shrill the chorus, drunk with din;
'We're sure the Kaiser loves our dear old Tanks!'

I'd like to see a Tank come down the stalls,
Lurching to rag-time tunes, or 'Home, sweet Home',
And there'd be no more jokes in Music-halls
To mock the riddled corpses round Bapaume.

2. German

The silence spreads. I talk and must talk. So I speak to him: 'Comrade, I did not want to kill you. If you jumped in here again, I would not do it, if you would be sensible too. But you were only an idea to me before, an abstraction that lived in my mind and called forth its appropriate response. It was the abstraction I stabbed. But now, for the first time, I see you are a man like me. I thought of your hand-grenades, your bayonet, of your rifle; now I see your wife and your face and our fellowship. Forgive me, comrade. We always see it too late. Why do they never tell us you are poor devils like us, that your mothers are just as anxious as ours, and that we have the same fear of death, and the same dying and the same agony - forgive me, comrade; how could you be my enemy? If we threw away these rifles and this uniform you could be my brother, just like Kat and Albert. Take twenty years of my life, comrade, and stand up - take more, for I do not know what I can even attempt to do with it now.

Erich Maria Remarque

(First World War German infantryman and author of *All Quiet on the Western Front*)

3. Elveden

It is nearly 100 years since the tanks departed. The training ground returned to farmland long ago. Yet even now the wind sometimes carries the sound of machine guns from a British Army firing range a few miles away. And from time to time the roar of American fighter planes tears the sky.

No one, it seems, hears the voices of Siegfried Sassoon and Erich Maria Remarque.

Remembering

Second Lieutenant Douglas Layman, 17th Battalion, Lancashire Fusiliers, killed in action on 22nd February 1916 aged 22 and resting in Bethune Town Cemetery and his comrade and batman, Private Albert Townsend, also of the 17th Battalion, killed in action at Bernafay Wood on 22nd July 1916, whose name is inscribed on the Thiepval Memorial to those who have no known grave.

FOOTNOTES AND SOURCES

(Where there are two or more references to a named source, details of only the first such reference to that source are given below.)

One: The Birth of the Tank

(1) *Tanks 1914-1918: The Logbook of a Pioneer* by Lieutenant Colonel Sir Albert G. Stern KBE CMG: Hodder and Stoughton, London : 1919

(2) *War Memoirs of David Lloyd George*: Odhams Press Limited, London: 1933-1938

(3) *Eyewitness: Personal Reminiscences of Certain Phases of the Great War*: Lt. Col. E. D. Swinton: Hodder and Stoughton, London: 1932

Two: The Men

(1) Documents relating to Lt. Victor Huffam held within papers of Captain Sir Basil Liddell Hart, Liddell Hart Centre for Military Archives, King's College, London

(2) Website: www.thefirsttankcrews.com/: Hosted by Mr Stephen Pope

(3) Sgt. Robert Parker: Imperial War Museum interview 1974: sound recording: Catalogue no. 492

Three: The Search for the 'Battlefield'

(1) *A Short Historical Guide to the Ancient Borough of Thetford*: W.G. Clarke: W. Boughton & Sons, Thetford: 1908

(2) *The Tank Corps*: Major Clough Williams-Ellis M.C. and A. Williams-Ellis, with an Introduction by Major-General H. J. Elles C.B., D.S.O.: From edition published in USA by George H. Doran Company: 1919

Five: The Men and the Machines

(1) Papers held at Bovington Tank Museum in relation to Elveden Explosive Area

(2) *Tank Warfare*: Captain Frank Mitchell M.C.: Thomas Nelson & Sons Ltd, London: Undated (probably 1920- 1930)

(3) Reminiscences of My Experiences in the First Tanks: W.T. Dawson : Papers held at Bovington Tank Museum.

(4) Account by Captain Groves: Papers held by Bovington Tank Museum

(5) *A Company of Tanks*: Captain W. H. L. Watson-Wilson D.S.O., D.C.M.: William Blackwood & Sons, Edinburgh and London : 1920

Six: Elveden - training and experiments

(1) Quoted in *The Tank Corps* by Williams-Ellis (as above, Chapter 3)

(2) *Life in a Tank*: Richard Haigh M.C.: From edition published in USA by Houghton Mifflin Company: 1918

(3) Quoted in *Tank Men* by Robert Kershaw: Hodder and Stoughton: 2008

(4) Horace Leslie Birks: Imperial War Museum interview 1976: sound recording: Catalogue No. 870

(5) Copy held at Bovington Tank Museum

(6) Quoted in Band of Brigands by Christy Campbell: Harper Perrenial: 2008

(7) *Tanks in the Great War*: Colonel J. F. C. Fuller: from USA edition published by E. P. Dutton and Co. New York: 1920

Seven: Rest and Relaxation (though not very much)

(1) Gunner Ernest Thwaites: Quoted in Band of Brigands by Christy Campbell: Harper Perennial 2008

Nine: A Difference of Opinion

(1) Liddell Hart papers, Liddell Hart Centre for Military Archives: King's College, London

Twelve: Arrival in France

(1) Private Horace Calvert: Imperial War Museum interview 1987: Catalogue No. 9955

(2) The War Diaries of Field Marshall Earl Haig: Original held as part of Haig Papers: National Library of Scotland

(3) *Tommy Goes to War*: Malcolm Brown: Tempus Publishing: 1999

Thirteen: Into Battle

(1) *The Tanks At Flers*: Trevor Pidgeon: Fairmile Books: 1995

(2) Ibid.

(3) *Somme*: Lyn Macdonald: Michael Joseph: 1983

(4) Imperial War Museum Documents: RSM Price: IWM Ref   82/22/11

(5) Amsterdam Correspondent of the London *Times*, 25/10/1916 quoting *Dusseldorfer Generalanzeiger* (German newspaper)

(6) *Flers & Gueudecourt*: Trevor Pidgeon: Leo Cooper : 2002

(7) War Diary, 5th Infantry Regiment, Bavarian War archives

(8) *Tommy Goes to War*: Malcolm Brown: Tempus Publishing: 1999

(9) *History of 211th Prussian Infantry Regiment*: Hans Fuhrman

Fourteen: The First Tank Action outside Europe

(1) *The Tank in Action*:   Captain D. G. Brown M.C.:   William Blackwood & Sons: 1920

(2) *Through Palestine with the 20th Machine Gun Squadron*: Anonymous author: printed and published for private circulation: 1920

PICTURE CREDITS:

Pages

8, 16, 65, 98, 128, Wikipedia
11, J.F.C. Fuller
23, vintagescript.blogspot.com
25, 32, 52, 70, 77, 78, Suffolk Record Office
27, blue-pelican-railway/flickr
29, Daniel Tatnell
31, 52, 63, 67, David Addy, St. Edmundsbury Chronicle website
25, 35, 45, 46, 47, 54, 112, 125 Author
40, 44, Tank Museum, Bovington
85, Rod Collins
98, Mme. M. Bellemain
106, Australian Government
108, Imperial War Museum
115, Untraced
122, Australian War Memorial Archive
130, www.1914-18.net

The author most gratefully acknowledges the written accounts drawn on in the compilation of this book. These are to be found specified in the footnotes section on page 142. Lastly, he wishes to express his sincere thanks to the persons and organisations who have particularly assisted him – the fact that these bring up the rear is a reversal of their true position! Any person or organization omitted is kindly requested to contact the author, who will readily endeavour to rectify matters in any future edition.